Leaving 1203

Leaving 1203

Emptying a Home, Filling the Heart

Marietta McCarty

Published by The Philosophy Shop

ISBN: 978-0-9998151-0-6

Cover photo © 2018 David Heald

Design © 2018 Roger Cunningham and Daniel Mason

Author photograph © 2016 Chuck Shifflett

www.mariettamccarty.com

Memoir / Personal Growth

FOR ALL OF US

"There is a crack in everything / That's how the light gets in."

Leonard Cohen, "Anthem"

CONTENTS

INTRODUCTION

The story of home is one that everyone knows, and it waits, with its memories and lessons, to come alive again.

Leaving 1203 is a love story of a house and its inhabitants. This simple home on a hill won the soulful appreciation of all the lives sheltered under its slate roof and within its brick walls. It was our refuge when happy or sad, anxious or calm, sick or well, young or old.

Imagine the heart-tugging responsibility of emptying this home. My mother gave me this job that would begin with her death in March 2013. My work on site commenced two months later after her May memorial garden party at 1203. So many things, so many memories, so many lives interwoven here for fifty-six years—what to do, not only with tangible objects but also with the varied emotions competing for space in my heart.

Setting out on my dreaded emptying project, slowly and at first imperceptibly, I felt a warming satisfaction boost my spirit. I was taken aback—how mysterious this subtle joy tangled up with yearning. I started to rely on this inexplicable contentment, trusting in its staying power. Though overwhelmed by the magnitude of the work in front of me, I gained strength as the goodness of the past wrapped around me. Like the women in my family before me, I put one foot in front of another, trusting in what my heart silently knew.

A no-frills girl of some repute, generally unmoved by acquisition and possessions, I suddenly found everything invaluable, priceless. The teacup, socks, suet container, bottle opener, hammer, all of it, every item represented hands that touched it, swung or sipped from it, toiled or played with it. My intense awareness of each thing before me in the summer of 2013 brought it back to life, present all over again. The grill and baseball bat—durable goods symbolizing enduring relationship—and childhood chums as alive in the house as current pals helping me lift wingback chair and braided rug. What a good place, then and now.

A little story sheds light on the charm of a house called home by four generations. Not only was I the hot-shooting (freshman!) starting guard on my high school basketball team, but juniors and seniors quickly offered me a lift home after games and practices. How awesome was I, number 21, hitching a ride with these campus stars. Arriving home supposedly to drop me off, everyone tumbled from a packed car without a thought—bursting through the back door, laughing and gabbing with my parents June and Mac, reserving a back slap or quick elbow for my brother Patrick. Leaving 1203, guests always received an escort to their cars plus a McCarty's keen oversight as they backed down the challenging driveway. The departed announced their safe navigation and farewell with a *beep-beep* of the horn. One evening as I walked my teammates back to the car, Betty Lou set me straight with this sobering fact of my youth: "All of us love coming over to your house and hanging around with your parents—they are so cool and we feel right at home. We're having a sleepover at the end of the season." (Did Betty Lou think I'd pass her the ball if I had *any* other option?)

That undeniable 1203 magnetism lured younger and older, long-time and first-time friends to its final three-month house party. What a grand collection of big-hearted folks showed up to help. My first cousins goofed around with neighborhood teenagers. A caregiver's grandkids exchanged phone numbers with my friends making day trips from Charlottesville. One day my former college students appeared, the next day my college roommate. My parents' friends brought family members, helpers brought their neighbors. My mother's and now my adored dog Billy, a West Highland Terrier, stayed by my side every day. Last in our spoiled canine lineage, Billy stole hearts and wagged us forward. Instant, easy camaraderie blossomed among people of all ages and backgrounds, sparking their desire to return and lend a hand. I was the grateful recipient of unsought help—a swimmer in a reservoir of sheer good will.

When we first called this spot home in 1957, who could have predicted all the shoulders rubbing together, all the people drifting comfortably through for a short stay or forever? All of us real human beings with our faults and strengths, off days and way on days, everyone bundled together in a safe house. I had long known all the characters, but never enjoyed the privilege of taking in the entire play until I stepped back and observed—pausing, reflecting, admiring, loving—all the while returning to the gradually emptying home.

Ownership of the 1203 "theater" was changing hands, and the main cast members sashayed out for a final curtain call, our joined lives now coming full circle: my father the swashbuckling lifeguard, my mother that jitterbugging swinger, my brother practicing chords from Bob Dylan's tunes, my aunt and uncle dropping off their four giddy hide-and-seekers for "summer camp," my grandmother Plum driving all night from Florida to surprise me at sunrise, my grandfather Big Daddy hitting pop flies just out of reach, friends near and far. Like watching the pieces of a puzzle fit at last, I absorbed this one extraordinary story of ordinary people.

What indescribable joy to experience recovery in the midst of loss. Hot and sweaty, teary and aggravated, I was also happy and invigorated. An overarching wellspring of hope sustained me. I heard a whispered promise that my life would be forever enriched.

Each chapter centers on physical objects as we discover secrets inside a messenger bag and read fine print with a magnifying glass. Baseball bats knock the ball out of the park. Food for body and soul sizzles in cast iron skillets. We form a friendship, the reader and I, detectives teaming up to ferret out treasures—the things that prompt rediscovery of truths tucked deep in our hearts. The book, our joint "research" project, digs into the places that call us home and rewinds the times of our lives.

What do I wish for readers? I wish for them the welcoming sound of voices calling them, too, back home again, a renewed sense of belonging, and reassurance that leave-takings and losses come with unexpected rewards as well. I let them in on what I did with everything in the house, why, and how.

1203 excelled at its last job. The old home served as a gentle yet powerful teacher, its walls and windows sometimes murmuring and at other times shouting the core lessons for good living. While readying for new dwellers, it delivered an unforgettable refresher course in the things that really matter—relationship, generosity, gratitude, courage, simplicity, sacrifice, hospitality, joy, perseverance, relaxation, responsibility, humor, humility. Timeless truths, trusty guides for wellbeing, now keepsakes forever.

Broken hearts open wider. Hearts split by love, longing, and separation heal stronger and wiser. I gained a more intimate understanding of the people who knew and loved me first. If possible, I love them even more.

Home emptier was the best paying, most rewarding job of my life.

CAST OF CHARACTERS

Residents
Marietta
June and Mac, my parents
Patrick, my brother

Regulars
Plum, my grandmother,
mother of June and Emma Jeanne (EJ)
EJ, my aunt and June's sister
Roger, my uncle and EJ's husband
Daniel, Maria, Jonathan, and Matthew, my first cousins
Big Daddy, my grandfather, Plum's first husband

Time: December 1957 - August 2013

Place: 1203, a Cape-Cod style, three-bedroom house sits atop three-quarters of an acre on a short dead-end street in Richmond's West End. Much of the property consists of a steep, partly-wooded front yard chock full of oaks and pines, Virginia's pink and white dogwoods, magnolia trees and wild azaleas. Built in 1942 on a narrow street bordered by deep ditches in a secluded area not far from the University of Richmond, it has the feel of a forested hideaway.

The Tin Milkbox, Broom, and Painted Heart

I headed home to the house that raised me. Sunrise shedding light on lime green leaves prompted my dawn departure from Charlottesville. I picked a beautiful day to make this difficult journey—my first trip home as house emptier.

Sleepy Billy awakened gradually, high-stepping in morning dew, dozing as soon as he settled into the passenger seat. The sun rose straight ahead as I relaxed into the routine of my most-traveled route, and before I knew it Billy shook himself awake. I exited the interstate.

Slowing for the right turn into the driveway, I instinctively beeped the horn. Heartsick, I jerked my hand from the steering wheel and braked to a full stop. No one expected tail-wagging Billy and lonesome me. I borrowed Billy's happiness and started anew up the driveway, each memorized bump a balm for my heart. The thrum of this one-of-a-kind ride soothed me—the motor steadily accelerating, car swerving around mini-potholes, the driver carefully angling to a stop in front of the garage—home again. I gazed over Billy's head out the car window, gladdened at the sight of the white picket gate opening onto the patio.

Making a slow entrance, I pulled magazines and a stack of envelopes from the mailbox outside the gate. Wrapped around the gate and dangling one above the other from a strand of twine woven through their rings, three delicately tapered blue-green bells clunked their distinctive low-key hello. I released the tiny hook inside the picket opening. Sagging on worn-out hinges, it inched back. I counted on the old-fashioned back stoop comfort waiting for me ten paces away.

Crossing from gate to stoop, I walked along a boxwood border and wondered how many feet had beaten this short path. Unless you were a lost traveler, a soon-to-be-disappointed salesperson, or a boy on our first date, 1203's entry was through the back door. Billy and I stood on the four by six-foot rectangular stoop. Two front pillars supported the slate overhang, slatted railings ran along each side, and screen and wood doors centered the space. Fifty-six years later, these last footsteps home hadn't lost their charm.

Tossing Billy's leash on a stoop railing and filling his outdoor water bowl from the hose, I faced the back of the house. The stoop cast a spell on me. As long as I can remember, three fixtures defined this 1203 landing pad—a milkbox, a broom, and a painted wood heart. The tin box won its permanent spot at the front of the left railing, visible from the gate for easy drop-offs. One tattered broom after another, each worn to a pronounced slant, leaned against the wall by the door. Fastened into the brick high above the right railing, the gray-blue heart hung at a slight tilt, its color fading over time. Billy stretched full length and flat as possible, taking advantage of the stoop's shaded cement for optimum belly cooling.

From the start, the small stoop drew a crowd. June sipped coffee with neighbors. Mac joined any child for a cloud game, pointing out lookalikes overhead—this cloud a guitar, that one a fox—and watching as the arrow or pig lost its shape and the cloud disappeared. I hung around with a book in one hand and a dog's chin in the other, waited for the mail, listened for a friend, or did nothing at all.

I felt new stirrings of old wisdom.

How I loved this trodden history book, record-keeper of fifty-six years of arrivals and departures. Long ago I delayed the walk to the bus stop, dallying on my covered outdoor lounge. I laced and re-laced my saddle shoes, dutifully shook the doormat, tried to think of something I'd forgotten. Today I stayed put. Here I might find some advice for 1203's reluctant emptier.

I flipped the milkbox lid up and down, up and down, each deliberate movement evoking images of fresh milk, eggs, and butter. Though the deliveries stopped shortly after we moved in, the versatile tin milkbox never budged. It protected newspapers from rain and dog treats from dogs. The neighborhood drugstore and mail carriers used it as a safety deposit box. Grownups, overloaded grocery bags in both arms, righted their imbalance by propping a foot on the makeshift tin stool. Turning the milkbox into a storage bin for birdseed proved its longest-lasting repurposing, a coffee cup for filling feeders buried in the mix. The spare key for a rarely locked backdoor "hid" in the birdseed, and a heart-shaped rock secured the top from smart squirrels. Best of all, it always provided a perch for short birdwatchers.

While most kids plopped on the milkbox for a time out from play, my four cousins thought it an entertainment center, especially the youngest. Four-year old Matthew reveled in uninterrupted summertime from his observation deck. He sat, lost in birdland, for hours. Birds chirped on branches, nibbled at feeders, scampered about the patio, bathed without being asked. I learned to pay attention, too, just like the littlest birdwatcher. Imitating birdcalls, we joined the choir of Virginia's red cardinals.

All the while—all my childhood and all my trips home—birds whistled and pranced. Bluebirds departed their tall house on a post and hopped on windowsills. Mourning doves surveyed their terrain and pecked at the ground. Woodpeckers sculpted rat-a-tat etchings into trees large and small. The birds had seduced me over the years with their singing communication and mesmerizing routines. Robin and blue-jay music hummed unconsciously within me through the years, and the whole orchestra reunited this morning to serenade Billy and me.

Different winged teachers from those of my youth but trilling the same old peaceful love song, they lured me into their domain, welcoming me back. Finches and cardinals flew away with my worries, and I felt increasingly carefree. Birds sang of old stoop truths—serenity in stillness, rejuvenation in silence, clarity in solitude. The quieter my mind, the louder and livelier their world. Their brilliant colors brightened my outlook—dancing sentries, posted on fences and treetops, overseeing my hard trip home.

I toured the backyard and looked back at the stoop for further instruction. A broom, frayed and misshapen of course, suggested a familiar activity. I started to sweep, envisioning loved hands on countless broom handles.

Generations of patio sweepers pivoted away from strong-jawed pups pursuing the flying, bristly object. June swept while waiting for company. Late in his life, Big Daddy chose his chore when he came to live with us—unasked, he cleared the patio of leaves and birdseed, paying his "rent" with a broom. Whenever I was sad or worried in my grownup years, I relied on the tempo of this loose-limbed motion. Sweeping under the old oaks calmed and uplifted my spirit, then and now. A lone sunflower's missing seeds formed a wide grin. How poignant on this morning the sweet sound of children at play, their shouts and laughter indistinguishable from those of my childhood. The nearby church bells tolled at the top of the hour. Then, all quiet. Suddenly the white-throated sparrow struck up the band. I swept and paid close attention. Back stoop memories floated into view.

I drop my book bag on the cement, sliding down a railing with a popsicle in hand, blanketing first pup Patches in the pleats of my school uniform skirt. The glow from the stoop's ceiling light illuminates the face at the kitchen window, and an unexpected visitor flings open the door with outstretched arms. Other surprises delight—special delivery packages, a turquoise hula hoop, soon-gobbled Rice Krispies treats from Mrs. Jones next door.

A glance at dreaming Billy and I giggled at the most fabled stoop story. June preferred champagne toasts for marking special occasions, especially reunions with her niece Maria. In cold months my mother chilled the bottle on the back stoop, but not on Billy's big night. Stumped by the disappearance of their half-full bottle of champagne, June and Maria called me for ideas—what on earth? They acted on my suggestion to open another bottle, but the vanishing of bottle one nagged at them. Days later, the yardman solved the mystery, picking up the now uncorked bottle in a flowerbed. Party-pooping Billy had dragged it from the stoop into backyard darkness.

Bringing the champagne thief over to swing with me on the glider, I thought how true to its message the old painted heart had stayed. It beckoned please come in as it also bid friendly adieu. It struck me that the chipped heart made its point like the birds and broom—simply, wordlessly.

Sounds of the mail truck puttering up the driveway, coupled with Billy's guttural response, broke the stoop spell. After chatting and thanking the carrier for years of personalized service, I waved

Billy's nemesis off. Leaning against my car, Billy on a leash, both of us looked down the driveway. For over a half century, this driveway had recorded all the up and down tire tracks, every coming and going tattooed on blacktop. I pictured our succession of dogs loping up the hill—Patches, Mink, Sheba, Tiger, Chico, Billy—primed for pats and treats.

Out of a happy nowhere, I beheld a knight in shining tinfoil armor stride up the driveway, wielding his mighty stick—five-year-old cousin Jonathan in shorts and sandals, his cardboard crown askew, triumphant over invading dragons. I thought about Jonathan's long relationship with the driveway. Swapping knighthood for college, he always stopped to see June and Mac at 1203 on the way to and from Chapel Hill. I learned from Jonathan, not my parents, about his almost drive-through the sunporch on a quick drive-by visit in 1981. "You know me, I always tried to 'leave-em-laughin' when June and Mac came out to the driveway to see me off. I delivered some quip and then whipped the car into reverse to head down the hill. The four posts protecting the sunporch from cars? Knocked one down with my right front fender. June smiled. Mac smiled. As always, they sent me on my way without any burden of bad feelings."

Years passed, and June and Mac headed down the driveway for middle-of-the night meetings with their gallivanting nephew. The threesome designated a pancake house off I-95 the rendezvous spot. After Mac died, June drove solo down the drive to treat Jonathan to pancakes. More years passed, and Jonathan brought his two-year-old daughter Hope for her one visit to 1203. Photographs captured her teetering walk down the old driveway, her determined circling at the bottom, and Hope heading back up, homeward bound.

The church bells announced the eleven-o'clock hour. I got it. I knew how to approach home emptying, even though I had no plan. I would rely on today's back-stoop lessons. How invigorating it was, just sitting. How necessary the solitary ride, this first time, from Charlottesville to Richmond, and how tranquil my morning solitude.

Stay in the present moment with us, the birds warbled. Swing steadily like a pendulum, the old broom suggested. Hide champagne bottles from Billy, the painted heart cheered me on. Wherever home emptying takes me in body and spirit, I'll let the old ways lead. This is plenty—this is enough.

Let's go for a walk, Billy. Then we'll get started.

The magnified newspaper clipping reads:

OPINION
By E.B. WHITE
'Choked ... n Laughter ...ain'

I ACCEPT the committee's award with thanks and with as much vain-glory as I can muster at so great a distance. I'm very unhappy about not attending the meeting. Ten years ago they pulled the railroad out from under me, and this almost severed my connection with New York. Then 16 months ago, I met with a motor accident, and this made the highway a problem for me. As for the skies, I quit using the flying machines in 1929 after the pilot of one of them, blinded

Flights of this sort of every good writer: the surrender to Probability, fin flaming denouement, wracked laughter — or with tears.
   Today, with so much of earth damaged and endangered, with so much of life dispiriting or joyless, a writer's courage can easily fail him. I feel this daily. In the face of so much bad news, how does one sustain one's

A Magnifying Glass and a Newspaper Clipping

On my first official afternoon as home emptier, I opted out of the job. Billy and I would take a step back and enjoy a brief vacation—a last chance to spend a day and night at home.

1203 exuded the spirit of its people—it embodied our lives at every stage. What did the telltale house have in store for me today? How would it feel? I was oddly eager to find out—seeing and absorbing as if for the first time.

Coming up the driveway after our walk, I looked at the front of the house. Our dream house with red brick and white shutters and trim in 1957 now presented itself with soft yellow brick and chocolate shutters and gray-blue trim—the old screen porch transformed into a sunporch, the tiny den doubled in size and windows. My escort and I walked up four mossy brick steps to the front stoop. I respectfully pulled down on the handle of the screen door and we hastened inside, soaking up the reassuring warmth of home.

Master of the first floor that he patrolled for almost fourteen years, Billy led the way. Still missing my mother, he took off for the rooms where they spent the most time. We started our tour on the sunporch, the spot for breakfast and reading the morning newspaper. What a cozy lair, open on three sides but partially-hidden by vines and bushes from the driveway—a glider and a couch, footstools and small tables, slews of magazines and framed photographs. A watercolor, capturing the house and front yard in 1980, hung from the brick wall over a tall, slender bookcase. As Billy inspected the sisal rug for any and all edibles, I relaxed in a wicker rocker. Except birdsong, all quiet. So far, same old good.

At Billy's command we took off for the other side of the house, trotting on pine floors through living and dining rooms to the den. The tiny half bath in the den gained a walk-in shower when Big Daddy's address changed to 1203. Three big windows, a long sofa and wing chairs, television and cd player—a room for watching tennis matches and baseball games, reading anything and writing notes, delighting in impromptu lunches and late-night movies, partying and napping. I lounged in my mother's chair, leaning back on her pillow knitted with the silhouette of Groucho Marx.

Looking at Billy looking at me, I was struck by how lucky we were to have called this place home. 1203's story, inseparable from mine, the house and I like kin. Far from alone, I sensed that those who'd been part of our fifty-six years had my back.

I needed to stay moving, one step ahead of emptying sorrow on my day off. In the kitchen, Billy lapped water and crunched food, ready for a snooze. I looked forward to keeping the kitchen alive all summer—the homiest room in the house, full of mismatched everything and unmatched good food and music.

Continuing my house tour at a lazy pace, I vacationed in the living and dining rooms. Stories lurked in the creaks of rockers, between cushions, in threads of Oriental rugs. The most "formal" areas in a house that radiated an upbeat, informal elegance, these were the only rooms without ceiling fans. In no way highfalutin, these spaces used for entertaining issued a vibrant welcome. I ambled back and forth between the two rooms, refreshing my sense of this place. Picking up a magnifying glass from a window sill, I pictured my mother peering at fine print or a stubborn splinter. Discreetly placed behind curtains, wrought iron bars supported open windows with worn sashes. Pie stands complemented three-legged tables. I recognized some old faithfuls from my earliest memories—a multiuse hutch whose bottom half opened with a key, the funnily-named dry sink, mirrors and paintings, a milkstool and cobbler's benches.

Brass candlesticks, with winged cherubs lifting high the candle holders, anchored the mantel, while four watercolors of Italy brightened the opposite wall—standbys from June's trip abroad to visit her sister EJ in Rome. Here, big trays on tripod legs, Portuguese candlesticks converted into lamps—there, handheld fans on end tables, and children's blocks atop bookcases. Benches in front of windows, prime spots for garden viewing, could be lifted easily to accommodate a gathering. Vases of fresh flowers always made the old things seem new. Both rooms retained their festive mood for a spontaneous celebration.

While picnicking with Billy and birds on the back patio, I noticed "Big Ben" protruding from the upstairs hall window. Silent on this pleasant day in May, our old air conditioner reliably cooled the whole house, helped along by closed doors, smothered cracks, and slanted blinds. Rumbling Ben's lone assistant was a portable window unit in the half bath window. Having grabbed my luggage from the car, I carried it in the direction of my favorite window in the house.

I headed up the fourteen pine steps, noting as ever the large knot in the seventh step that signaled the halfway point. At the landing I admired the stained glass installed in the window above the legendary air conditioner. My preferred upstairs view drew me right away to the bathroom. I loved this window through which early morning sun proclaimed a new day. It looked out over the backyard almost as far as the much-traveled road that ran parallel to our dead-end street. The beeps of cars and loud hiccups of old mufflers occasionally floated through an open window—a big world awaited as we snuggled among big trees. Today the smells of fresh-mown grass permeated the upstairs, neighbors on both sides contributing to the aroma.

This final summer at 1203, I would bunk in Patrick's first bedroom on the backside of the house. The smallest bedroom with the fewest emptying challenges, it would be a simple task to pack up its contents toward the end of my job. A bookcase at the foot of a single bed, a dresser and bedside table, one straight back chair—the room promised me an uncluttered retreat. I dropped my canvas bag on the chair.

My childhood bedroom adjoined Patrick's on the same side of the stairwell. It became first Big Daddy's in 1979, then Plum's bedroom in 1996, and EJ's domain thereafter whenever she visited. Guests gravitated to this room as well and its character and allure hit me once again. My schoolgirl desk tucked into the nook created by the front dormer window. The shrieks of giddy kids, playing in the yard at 1201, rode in on the wind. In an instant, I treated myself to an upgrade, choosing to spend my vacation night right here. A breeze ruffled the bottom of a slightly tattered curtain at the small bedside window, the sound assuring sweet dreams.

Crossing the hall to my parents' room, I couldn't resist a peek in the linen closet. Quite an amazing collection on the door bulged from a hidden hook—jackets, raingear, sweaters of all sizes and styles, a dog leash. The closet smelled the same—clean sheets and towels and blankets, long-stored and seldom-aired. I left the door ajar, a chance to add that fresh grass smell to the mix.

Photographs of Mac abounded in June's bedroom. Another drop-front desk, similar to mine, nestled under the dormer window in this room, too. Pillows for late night reading propped against the headboard of her Jenny Lind bed, a down comforter at the foot, a heating pad readied for back relief. I perched rebelliously on the edge of her bed, heedless of a lifetime's admonitions not to sit on the side of a bed, and focused on her aged-oak bedside table. A rotary phone, a wedding gift from a previous beau and retrofitted with adapter plugs, covered the bottom shelf. Untangling the long, curling phone cord, I listened to the authoritative drone of the dial tone, a kid about to sneak a forbidden call. A nail file and a few bobby pins, a small white notepad and stubby pencil, and an Elmore Leonard book were strewn about the tabletop, its four sharp edges sanded round by time.

I burst out laughing at the image of Cleopatra reclining in this bed! The long handle of an eerie mask leaned against the table, easily reached by a late-night prankster, octogenarian June at play.

Pulling the delicate latch on the drawer beneath the phone, I fingered combs, scissors, Kleenex packets, cough drops, sheets from her notepads. I found grocery lists, tasks for the yardman, well-intentioned phone call reminders. Several pieces of paper, carefully creased, caught my eye—my mother's penciled titles of her favorite movies. A film buff extraordinaire, she whispered a special line along with the actor, pointed out nuanced movement or expression, identified unheralded actors. I noted ones we'd watched together. *Born Yesterday, Suspicion, Rebecca, Zulu* ("You're a better man than I am, Gunga Din"). Of course, *My Cousin Vinny, Sounder, The Great Escape, Mr. Blandings Builds His Dreamhouse.* Yes, *Roman Holiday, Frankenstein, Laura, Norma Rae.* Surely, *Spartacus, Gaslight, Maytime, Jezebel.* And, *Hurricane, The Client, Gloria,* and *Casablanca* ("Of all the gin joints in all the towns in all the world, she walks into mine"). She'd double-underlined our annual flick, *An Affair to Remember* ("If you can paint, I can walk—anything can happen, don't you think?").

The entire house felt lived in. Sweet, glad awareness came over me. The old home had surprises waiting for its remaining resident, secrets to share with its emptier—new insights about those nearest my heart.

Poking around upstairs, I chose books for my summer reading, leaving a selection on my bedside table. Thinking back on my day thus far, I realized the primacy of books for all of us at 1203—bookcases in every single room, bookends on tables, books in cupboards, books on any shelf. We read books like crazy, each of us with our own stash—I couldn't wait to get my high school summer reading list of thirty books. I'd fallen in love with the written word while sounding out my first ones in a big-print collection called *The Treasure Box*. Mac's prizes included his inscribed Edgar Cayce books, John Cheever short stories, and *How the Irish Saved Civilization*. I always found something new in June's oldies collection: a 1913 primer on *Just Being Happy* in which she used my birth announcement as her place keeper, a 1924 collection of *One Hundred and One Famous Poems*, and *Wuthering Heights*. Both parents possessed copies of Walt Whitman's *Leaves of Grass*.

I had set aside one of June's oft-read books for teatime reminiscences. I pored over EJ's handmade book of her own poems and photographs entitled *My Sister's Window*. She was right about June when she wrote in 2001 that "For her, everything is just as it was. Everyone is still out there in the garden. Memory is a peopled place." There is no place like home. I must take good care of this one, this summer.

Billy and I dozed in the den like real vacationers. Awakening, I knew instinctively where to go for real adventure. I had no specific expectations but sky-high hopes.

I saw it under the glider on the sunporch—a gray rectangular wood box with five bright red apples on a white background painted on its top, indentations on the sides for lifting. My mother's personal treasure box, its contents unknown to me, till now. Lid up. Mind blown.

Mamma Mia! Photographs, notes, clippings, a maze of delights born of June's penchant for safeguarding valuables. Her box marked the final exhibit of a master curator with impeccable taste—one who ignored organization by nature and on principle. I created piles of photographs, separated greeting cards from post-cards, letters from notes, and saved one special folder for last.

Time flew in a dizzying display. Many of the old photo-graphs I'd never seen—the bunch likely spanned a century and a half. I fetched the magnifying glass. Two adults and two girls pose on the slanting front porch of a cabin. Careful cursive on the back identifies the somber man with long beard and hair, the serious woman in a full-length dress and apron, the children barely hinting at smiles: Ruby Moring Williamson, my great-great-grandmother, stands alongside her younger sister Vergie with their parents, Emily Jane Nunnally Moring (1844-1916) and Floyd Caswell Moring (1842-1917). In another, Plum's "Papa" strolls at ocean's edge in his one-piece bathing suit. In two eerily similar photos, newborns Plum and Big Daddy rock in cradles. Seven and five-year-old June and EJ giggle as they balance on roller skates. My two-year-old dad sits in a row of little rascals, their names written on back. Both June and Mac trek reluctantly to their respective elementary schools, lugging book bags and frowning…now grin with their own high school buddies, flirtatious and playful…and soon enough, refined and gracious in formal garb, chaperone my prom.

One sequence, kept together in a small fragile envelope, brought me up tall. I'm a wobbling baby splashing in the river in Gloucester, Virginia, smiling with two front teeth while passed from one pair of outstretched arms to the next, held high and kissed on the cheek in each picture, tumbling among sand castles at the end. I was infused with sudden, startling pleasure that I had the respon-sibility of emptying this home. It's my time to return all that love.

Billy and I walked while I welcomed this shift in perspective—home emptying as opportunity. We picked up our pace for home, anticipating more sunporch loot.

I hesitated at the prospect of reading correspondence not intended, originally, for me—but soon jumped at the chance to know more about people I knew best. I eavesdropped tentatively, returning letters to envelopes and reinserting photos into cards—tearfully privy to tender exchanges. I pulled out several that belonged together in spirit.

In black ink calligraphy-like cursive, my father's dad courts his mother Bess on postcards dated September 10 and 20, 1915. I never got to know this grandfather who died when I was three, but he's alive today: "I have the writing spirit this morning. A brief toast to you, without coffee, and every word is true. Kiss and Love to you, Mac." His son Mac's anniversary card to June signed "Always love" dealt me an old blow. My pop draws his own header: "1944-1990." And then: "It has been fun and games, sweet and lovely – and always a wonderful experience with you and whatever you're up to. There's one and four and then there's more – years that is!" He lived just one more. Placed inside this card is a paper heart folded in half so that it would fit in Mac's wallet. June writes, "Thank you for a nice day. Be happy. Love."

Sent after his beloved Mac died, Jonathan's letter to June says a lot about all three. "I was so impressed, so proud of you, not only at the funeral but afterwards. Your composure and brightness – against all odds – was inspiring to me. Seeing you take it as it came, smiling and greeting people, and remembering that Mac stood for positive spirit and graciousness and reaching out, and not oversentimentality and darkness, really made me feel whole."

Jacqueline, lifelong friend of June and EJ, wrote to them when Plum died. "My favorite memory is one that happened some years ago. I drove toward Gloucester where Jennie had her cottage. Two women were walking along this country road, arms linked around each other's waists. When I got closer I saw that it was Plum and her sister Jennie. It was a charming picture then and especially now."

Fortunately, I saw another letter and photo good for a guaranteed laugh. Belle of the ball June stares up at a doting cadet from Virginia Military Institute in Lexington, Virginia. George didn't go down easy when she ended their courtship, and in a last plea he pens a postscript: "June, if you don't get this letter, please let me know." Thank you, George, for today's pick-me-up and for not being my father.

I reached for the overstuffed folder that Mac the wishful organizer had labeled "Lifestyles and Other Things," the surefire topper. June savored her seemingly random collection of hundreds of clippings that she often called her "autobiography." What a romp! A 1937 menu from the Miller & Rhoads Tea Room and a baby opossum sunning in a water dish. A rainbow over a ballpark during a rain delay and a rescued bluebird on a shoulder. Puppies in Christmas stockings and an ad for a Live-on-Stage, adults-only performance by Marsha Mellow. Several of Patrick's "Altered Takes" music reviews and Russell Baker's 1984 article "Eating with the Swells" about the pretensions of dining in Manhattan. Peacock feathers spread wide and reports of a rehabbing chimpanzee with a mental disorder. Two copies of the "Prayer to St. Jude," patron of lost causes, and poems by Mary Oliver, "The Summer Day," and Grace Paley, "On Occasion."

I pulled out two yellowing clippings. One I'd read in disbelief and would reread tonight. The other required the magnifying glass, and even so I squinted at the fading print of ageless baseball player Satchel Paige's tips for good living. "1. Avoid fried meats. They angry up the blood. 2. If your stomach disputes you, lie down and pacify it with cool thoughts. 3. Keep the juices flowing by jangling around gently as you move. 4. Go very lightly on the vices, such as carrying on in society. 5. Avoid running at all times. 6. Don't look back. Something might be gaining on you."

What a holiday. I turned off the front and back stoop lights. Tucked into my childhood bed, eyes as wide as Billy's, I read the second clipping again—E. B. White's acceptance speech for his 1971 National Medal for Literature. What struck my mother about his words?

"I have always felt that the first duty of a writer was to ascend—to make flights, carrying others along if he could manage it…. Despair is no good—for the writer, for anyone…. Only hope can carry us aloft, can keep us afloat…. Writing itself is an act of faith, nothing more. And it must be the writer, above all others, who keeps it alive."

Satchel, something might be gaining on me.

Work Gloves and Trowels, Gardens Everywhere

I awakened in my childhood bedroom to old-time, unrehearsed harmony. A surround sound of birdsong blowing through open windows heralded my first full day on the job. I'd picked the easy way out to tiptoe my hard way in to home emptying—Charlottesville pals joining 1203 neighbors for outdoor work and play.

Sipping coffee on the patio, I put aside the morning paper to take in the sights. Cotton work gloves waved at me from the pointy tips of the picket fence. Faded, floppy blue wristbands decorated most of the dirt-colored gloves, almost all with holes in the fingertips. Trowels lay on tables and poked out of planters. A wheelbarrow of mulch stood ready to roll. Flowers and bushes strutted about in flamboyant Spring finery. I leaned back in the recliner, thoughts focused on another time.

"A quarter for whoever spots the first jonquil!" Mac challenged his three housemates every end of February. Our private searches commenced, competitors alert for a tiny bud's yellow splash. We delighted year-round in nature's unfolding, our love of the earth as perennial as the flowers poking their faces through the soil each Spring. Summer guaranteed leafy shade from big oaks, crinkly pink and white blossoms atop the fetching, leggy bark of crape myrtles, and delicate roses beautiful by any name. Smitten by Autumn, my mother reveled in its crisp air and panorama of red, yellow, and orange leaves. She collected fallen lovelies—scattering them on tables and window sills—sealing too-spectacular-to-be-true leaves in wax paper and pressing them between pages of our heavy dictionary. Winter teased us with its promise of carefree "snow days" for Patrick and me, trading our books for sleds and warm milk and honey.

Far back as I remembered the world, the elemental pleasures of digging in the dirt enriched my family. In a classic black and white photograph, my father has been recruited for plowing duty—a spiffy gardener in dress shirt, trousers, and his prized two-tone, lace-up shoes. Sleeves rolled up, he bends over the wooden handles of a tiller with a smile for the camera. While we lived in our apartment, Big Daddy tended this garden that produced every possible vegetable for summer's table, enough for giveaways, and plenty for Plum's canning extravaganza. On my hands and knees or the seat of my pants scouting my weed-pulling beat—scooting from row to row, row after row—my excuses mounted as I begged to trade in my handheld hoe. Secretly, I got a kick out of my dirty-kneed job, turning cartwheels amidst cornstalks and string beans, arms outstretched in front of the sprinkler for a cooling waterfall.

Those were the days. Time to jumpstart this one, so Billy and I dogtrotted down the driveway for our morning walk. We came upon the creek, at almost the same time of day, where Patrick and I waited for the school bus. I imagined lugging a heavy book bag down the bus steps at school day's end, walking the familiar block home that I walked with Billy now. We stood at the crossroads of our short street, yellow caution signs bright as ever proclaiming "Dead-end Street" and "Children at Play." I still anticipated that first glimpse of the big oaks overseeing the second house on the right.

Today, I paid overdue attention to the flowering welcome along the street. Hardy day lilies and jonquils prospered in and around our ditch. Poking around this cheery, untended area, I heard the laughter of neighbors, trailing behind Billy and me, on a leisurely pace for 1203. Friends from Charlottesville squeezed their two vehicles into a rocky space carved into the yard near the bottom of the driveway. Railroad ties and azaleas formed the three-sided border of this tiny parking lot. Spontaneous conversations broke out as we made introductions and unloaded outdoor equipment. Garden tools swung over shoulders and work gloves wedged into pockets, we strolled up the driveway, identifying plants and shrubs while deciding on front-yard group work assignments. Raking leaves, clipping low-hanging dead limbs and adding them to a heap of already fallen branches, heavy pruning here and light trimming there. We lolled up the driveway, commenting on its reception line of forsythia and japonica bushes, sedum and lariope, azaleas and dogwood trees, gooseneck loosestrife and helter-skelter hyacinths.

At the top of the driveway, we walked along the slate path toward the front door. Only a few paces from the front stoop, four white chairs tucked under a matching round table centered a tiered patio of tiny rocks and slate—here, June and EJ honored their standing reservation for afternoon tea. Painted window boxes stuffed with petunias, impatiens, geraniums, and begonias rested on living and dining room sills. A meandering row of boxwood stretched the width of the house. Tall grasses in big urns and yellow and red knockout roses kept us company. A scattering of English boxwood, all propagated from small cuttings, completed our hilltop preserve. At the edge of this small, cared-for berm, a blast of color dazzled us—a thick, wild bank of white, pink, red, orange, and lavender azaleas.

While my soon-to-be helpers admired the scene from stoop and chairs, I remembered this space very differently. Early in our tenure truckloads of dirt established this crest, both for planting and erosion prevention—the steep drop-off from stoop to street transformed by grass and bushes, crocus and periwinkle, table and chairs, and human and canine socializing. The rest of the front yard stayed a wilderness for birds and squirrels, magnolias and dogwood, established oaks and pines.

We moseyed along the slate path back to the driveway. The old camellia bush protected the front side of the sun porch—its wintry, deep red blossoms a sign of Spring even amidst snowfall. Alongside the sun porch, clematis and morning glory vines scaled trellises abutting the glass, their roots sharing a bed with nasturtiums, ferns, and a cement statue of a child at play. Small flowerbeds blossomed to the left and right of the back gate, a sweeping arch over the gateway's entrance shaped by yellow Lady Banks roses.

What a worksite! Like kids on an Easter egg hunt, nine gardeners spread out over patio and yard. Bounty everywhere—assorted patches of flowers, shrubs, a Japanese maple here and a redbud tree there, a butterfly bush attracting its namesakes and its gardenia companion ripe with its unmistakable scent. In worn lettering, a stanza of Dorothy Frances Gurney's poem was inscribed on a black sign secured in one bed on a short pole: "The kiss of the sun for pardon / The song of the birds for mirth / One is nearer God's heart in a garden / Than anywhere else on earth." Rocks formed borders and big ones nestled in mulch. Along the length of the back fence a mature, winding garden, long ago tilled and planted from scratch with friends' housewarming gifts, symbolized time's passage.

After our morning to mid-afternoon spent lopping deadwood and separating bulbs, hauling tarps and dragging branches, talking and falling quiet, we picnicked on the front terrace. Items contributed by my team members complemented each other, unplanned—chilled soups, pasta salads, mint tea, fruit and chocolate. I waved farewell at the top of the driveway to my friends departing with brimming baskets of 1203 transplants—hosta, rabbit's ear, lily of the valley, lavender, rosemary, bleeding heart, iris, acuba, bulbs a-go-go.

I had a date with Billy. We headed for June's "secret garden," an area my helpers surely saw but somehow sensed to leave alone. This surprise patch lies behind and between two big boxwood bushes at the far end of the patio, this "secret" sown in the ground last and late in our time at 1203. The only stretch of uncultivated soil remaining—around the side of the house away from the drive-way—a space seldom used unless giving chase to an overthrown Frisbee or a runaway dog. From a tall window in the den, a cozy room sun-speckled all afternoon, June looked down at this exhibit of colorful vitality. Rose of Sharon and rhododendron, white daisies and jonquils for Mac, rosemary and oregano, a sundial telling time to a concrete angel, a birdbath and feeder, a rattan basket chair swinging amidst hanging baskets. Black-eyed-Susans provided escort along a pebbled, brick-bordered path to the picket gate where two boxwood closed rank on June's secret. The live-in gardener of 1203 since 1958, June's last garden patch brought her incomparable joy.

Billy and I called a time-out, two ne'er-do-wells lounging in this lush garden. Swinging in the basket chair, I understood as never before what this secluded three quarters of an acre represented to my parents, grandparents, and aunt when we took up residence at 1203. A part of the earth was ours for growing plants and planting trees and watching seeds sprout into vegetables. We relied on "our" dirt even more than the oil furnace or electricity. For all our love of the house, we bowed to the earth as our first home. What better companions than bees and phlox, fireflies and wisteria? The home on the hill snuggled into its environment—it belonged in its place. Like an oak extending its lifeline in the ground, a sensation of root-edness secured us, too, in nature's life-affirming rhythm.

When I awoke this morning, I was touched by the sight of an iconic 1987 photo in the collage under the glass top of the bedside table. Two twin left hands plant creeping thyme in cracks between cobblestones. Fingers of both slightly-arthritic hands scratch the dirt—if these hands weren't stored in my memory bank, I might think they belonged to one kneeling gardener. But I recognized the delicate, seldom-worn watch on one wrist and gold bracelet clasped shut on the other. June and EJ, sisters having at their favorite pastime.

I recognize rose and dogwood as gifted teachers because I inherited my forebears' reverence for the earth.

My grandmother and her girls swapped a lifetime of clippings, bulbs, and plants back and forth, unsought and always welcomed. A snip of basil and an offshoot of lilac, grafts from a holly bush and a mountain laurel, tomato plants and zinnia seeds, tulip and hydrangea bulbs moving among the threesome and filling a bucket of plenty for any game visitor. Lucky for us that Plum's daughters passed along their hands-in-the-dirt passion to their girls, my cousin Maria and me. We carry on this love affair with the natural world, our fingers replacing theirs, remembering. We've left gardens behind—Maria's planted with children at her boys' elementary schools and mine with philosophy students at my college. Maria investigates clouds and champions small seabirds. I rub rosemary on the way out the door and reposition rocks beneath tall grasses. I am easily awed by moss and lichen. I'd be lost without this primal relationship to the earth—unmoored without anchoring roots. Feeling affinity with nature and resonating with all life is heaven indeed.

Shored up like a brace-supported sapling, I resumed familiar outdoor activities. I looked forward to executing my childhood chores this summer—rotating plants for even sun exposure, reaching tall for window box watering, clipping an occasional branch, and pulling from an ultimately victorious crop of weeds. This small plot of land would deliver bittersweet joy all summer. And I wanted everything at its busting-green best for the new, unknown residents. It never looked better than right now, having been gussied up for June's early May memorial garden party.

Driving home to Charlottesville with Billy and my bundle of transplants, the smell of peppermint permeating the car, I thought about June's last garden bash. How best to celebrate June McCarty's kicky, happy life? She smiled when I suggested a backyard / patio garden party, though wondered about my (non-existent) rain plan. Never had the simple home on a hill shone as it did on that day—everything teeming with color on a sunny, cool afternoon. A tent covered most of the patio and backyard, room in the sunshine for some tables and chairs. "Am I on a movie set?" one properly-astonished guest enthused. Standing at tables and gathered on the patio, family and friends raised a glass of champagne to the lady of the house. Billy greeted arrivals, navigated around ankles without incident, and stretched out in the center the instant a circle formed. Good boy, Billy, my man of the house. With the party in full swing, he slipped away to the kitchen-in-chaos for unsupervised rummaging. Dog gone—barbecue too.

As I prepared for the party, I soaked up the simple beauty of the place. So much loveliness here had originated at other homes while so much of 1203 now roots in countless places, most I'll never know. Ah, the sturdy, unseen roots that bind.

June chose Richmond's Lewis Ginter Botanical Garden for those wishing to make a donation in her name. "I fell in love with that place the first time I saw it," she often said, and she managed a visit not long before she died. I sauntered with an old family friend through the Garden a few days after her party. The Children's Garden at Lewis Ginter benefitted from gifts in June's name, and what a thrill to hear ecstatic cries of child gardeners as we approached. Jan and I sat on a stone bench, rapt in splendor. "Look! Look!" a young horticulturist screamed for all to hear, her miniature trowel pointing the way to once-buried treasure.

Digging to be continued.

Cast-Iron Skillets and a Songbook

The unforgettable first morning in my new childhood home, I snapped awake at the whiffs of coffee wafting upstairs in a dark house, not knowing that the night before Mac had set a timed percolator for 6am. His ongoing late-night contribution aside, June reigned over the kitchen—the hub of activity and central hangout. The point of entry and exit, 1203's heart beat in this bustling eight-by-eleven-foot space. The aroma of home cooking had seeped into kitchen walls. Sounds of countless voices hovered. Its scuffed pine floor wore traces of everyone's footsteps.

The kitchen this early June morning in 2013 looked much like its usual self. A step up from the back stoop leads into the kitchen, the door's jingling sleigh bells announcing arrivals. Ladder back chairs surround a rustic, always-set table resting on a braided rug woven by June and Plum. A dough bowl heaped with fruit centers the table. Formica countertops beneath white wood cabinets surround the small, shallow double sink, a dish strainer on the sink's left side and soaking dishes on the right, a wash cloth drying on the faucet. A big window above the sink looks out onto the patio and backyard. Stationed above the window, a ceramic monkey posts lookout. Dishtowels drape over a goose's sculpted head attached to a nearby cabinet. An old cheese board etched "To Mac from Jon" props against the window sill. The sill's lineup features small pots of violets and fresh chives, teacups, and teensy wire chairs fashioned from the tops of champagne bottles. Taped recipes and a few of June's favorite quotes adorn the cabinets, instructions for preparing salmon mousse stuck between observations from D. H. Lawrence ("I never saw a wild thing feel sorry for itself") and Annie Dillard ("Spend the afternoon. You can't take it with you").

A smaller window, facing 1201, provides year-round smoke ventilation. Copper pans dangle from nails above the stove and cast-iron skillets rise in stacks on burners. Maria's annual gifts of her colorful handmade potholders lie atop an aged copper kettle. The fridge, covered with magnets, stands to the oven's right beside a swinging door that leads into the dining room. Small bookcases and tables line the wall opposite the back door. A hanging cattycornered oak cupboard bridges two walls, Billy's bed and bowls below. Among the cupboard's eclectic holdings, one casserole dish remains a hideaway for cash reserves. To the right of the door to the basement, a two-tiered, glass-fronted, old-timey dental cabinet stores partyware.

Eating cereal alone at the table, I reconstructed the hopping kitchen of yesteryear. Countertop mainstays include lemon, vinegar, olive oil, a pot of tea, and soft butter. Cast-iron skillets crackle with browning butter, sautéing garlic, caramelizing onions. Pots steam with Brunswick stew and spicy chili. Why did everything—anything—cooked up in this kitchen taste so good? Piping hot fried green tomatoes topped with ground pepper, cornbread and spoonbread, collard greens and baked beans, grilled cheese and mac'n cheese. Shrimp (cocktail and creole), omelets, and grits. Whole meal tuna salads with watercress and spinach, a tart vinaigrette complementing capers, sliced eggs, and veggies. I request Pomodoro, my favorite pasta sauce, and accept seconds of ratatouille. After beets and potatoes cool, June whips up two of her specialties—heart-shaped pickled beets and the world's best potato salad.

If only I could trade my now soggy cereal for the five-star breakfast of my youth. Nothing pleased the palate like chicken gravy ladled sparingly over small bits of toast. I understood the hard way, right away, the one seasoning essential to all 1203 home-cooking and longed for this missing ingredient—even the taste of gravy bread would be dulled without the spice of free-flowing conversation. Whether eating in the dining room for fancier meals and company or wedging around the kitchen table, we thrived on respectful conversation assured by the comfort of home cooking. We broke bread and talked, touching shoulders and knocking elbows, listening and locking eyes. With children always included in this unforced ritual, I feasted on the pairing of food with dialogue. Conversation around the dining and kitchen tables, whether lighthearted or serious, was different somehow. It mattered, napkins in laps, candles lit. Chicken roasted in a clay pot, complemented by mashed potatoes, enhanced a glasses-clinking celebration of my first return home from college. We relied on kitchen table closeness during the hardest times—this natural communion sustained the four of us on the evening we absorbed the shock of Mac's terminal diagnosis. During his remaining six weeks, we gathered here in unspoken solidarity.

Looking around the kitchen in morning quiet, I sensed the afterglow of countless conversations. I loved this room and resisted my morning resolution to empty it even a little. I sat at the table, ate an apple, peeled wax from a candlestick. Nothing doing.

I got up and fiddled around, absentmindedly peeking under the sink and into the oven. Deciding it was time to walk me, Billy stood at the back door. His leash hung on the pantry doorknob. The pantry! What an enticing target for today's emptying task, I thought, a small space in which I might accomplish something. I should have known better.

The tiniest room in the house, barely enough space for a twirl around, the pantry hid to the right of an open back door. "Get out of the pantry!" a vexed June yelled on cue from living room or den, but the pantry never failed to entertain. Its unknowability seduced me for fifty-six years. Pulling the string with a dangling plastic alligator at its end, the ceiling light revealed a mini-warehouse that appeared almost immediately upon our making a home of 1203—a can opener and pencil sharpener mounted on the wall, a peg board supporting an array of pots and pans, shelves packed. A bright splash of colors shone from jar after jar of my grandmother's canned goods: chow-chow, dilly beans, watermelon pickles, brandied peaches, succotash, tomatoes. June's row of cookbooks stretched wide—*From Julia Child's Kitchen, James Beard's Theory and Practice of Good Cooking,* and her dogeared Edna Lewis classic *The Taste of Southern Cooking.* Shelves bulged with pasta and rice in tin containers, carousels of canned goods and spices, bags of crackers and chips clipped with clothespins, colanders and cutting boards and vases. Bags of dog food and birdseed multiplied on the floor.

One cut-glass bowl, identified by its ever-tarnished silver rim, took me back. June filled this deep container with her acclaimed potato salad. For occasions, she molded her house special in the shape of a heart. Her signature dish doubled as June's get-well card, her potato salad delivered by hand or by Mac to someone sick, grieving, or homesick for 1203. I set the rimmed bowl on the kitchen table, resolving to recreate June's masterpiece.

Looking over the pantry, I picked up a large lacquered tray, small heart-shaped molds for pickled beets, and one of Plum's aprons. I realized how well and how often home cooking traveled—hospitality on the move. Mac and I delivered weekend suppers prepared by June to Mr. Woods, a delicious way of thanking the man who taught me to play tennis. Jars of beets left on a friend's doorstep served as June's tangy birthday greeting. After he moved into a nursing home, Big Daddy looked forward to Plum's twice daily delivery of her still warm home cooking. Plum's grandchildren honor her insistence never to return an empty bowl or platter to the giver of food. In her later years, Maria and Jonathan reciprocated June's homecooked hospitality—Maria's almost-warm gingerbread special-delivered from the west coast, and Jonathan's complete meals prepared in D.C. for the 1203 freezer guaranteed her the comfort of homemade food.

Examining an old radio retired to a top shelf, my mood brightened at the thought of June's contagious joy in music. She sang with or without radio accompaniment, a ready-for-showtime voice. She danced with or without partner—a smooth foxtrot and groovy cha-cha, her lively jitterbug pure class. With radios perched on window sills and on bedside tables, music of the Forties and Fifties reverberated around the house—cranking up the volume a post-apartment perk. During our early years the loudest musicians performed in the pantry, primitive speakers projecting the greatest hits. Leaning upright in cardboard sleeves, LP vinyl records filled two shelves on the left wall and surrounded a phonograph that spun the playlist of my youth. Stacked albums dropped one-by-one onto the velvet turntable, the phonograph arm lowered the needle, and bam! Ella Fitzgerald belted out *The Cole Porter Songbook*. Billie Holiday's "I Get a Kick Out of You" and Dinah Washington's "Manhattan" inspired singalongs. June crooned "Que Sera, Sera" in a pitch-perfect duet with Doris Day. We journeyed down Broadway with soundtracks from *South Pacific, The Music Man, West Side Story,* and *My Fair Lady*. I heard our old chums singing again this morning—Vic Damone touting "An Affair to Remember," Sarah Vaughan teasing "Let's Call the Whole Thing Off," Nat King Cole "Walkin' My Baby Back Home."

Idling, I returned to the kitchen table and thumbed through

a couple of cookbooks. My thoughts lingered on my mother the music woman, however. A clear pre-1203 memory shook loose. I wondered why my mother spent so much time making lists at the apartment kitchen counter, writing notes that she didn't share or discuss, then putting them away in a drawer. After interrogating Mac, Plum, and EJ separately and often, I believed their unanimous answer. "Your mother is writing songs," they confided. I didn't doubt for a second this disclosure that made me proud. I sat today in kitchen quiet, cobwebs fleeing, the past becoming present. Of course, my song and dance mother, also an aspiring songwriter. I remember her.

I see young June enchanted by another world, no radio playing, her focused, far-off gaze out the kitchen windows. Hips and head swung to a beat she alone heard. She tapped heel and toe, toe and heel—slow, slow, quick, quick. Whipping out a notepad, she scribbled fast, mouthed words and hummed, crossed-out rejected lines with a sigh. I observed the chef lost in thought, and lost to all else, until she returned pencil and pad to her special drawer.

Though I couldn't resist the pantry's pull, I stayed out of the drawer to the far right of the kitchen sink. June claimed it for her own and only. After checking it out on the sly a few times, the contents didn't tempt me anyway—lots of little notepads beneath stacks of dishtowels, left-handed scissors for her ambidextrous use only. The drawer gradually escaped my notice. Now a possible goldmine awaited. Please, old off-limits drawer, reward my self-control.

I never saw much less read a June song. Would I get my chance now? Betting on a long shot, I opened the drawer.

In perhaps my most excited home-emptying act, I gingerly dumped the contents of the drawer upside down on the countertop. Sheet music stuck like shelf paper on the bottom, and I interpreted the bright yellow cover of Duke Ellington's "Sophisticated

Lady" as a positive sign. I hesitated, respecting my mother's privacy, postponing disappointment. The items stashed closest to the Duke, now at the top of the pile, waited. I turned them over.

HOT DIGGETY DOG, Billy! Hit parade!

I ran fingers over hidden classics, most handwritten by June and a few typed by Mac, safeguarded inside a 1952 leather date-book. In kindergarten scrawl, I'd scratched through the name "June McCarty" and replaced it with "Cole Porter." I didn't recall this book or my inscription. Clearly the datebook belonged to my mother—the leather-bound relics smelled of her kitchen.

I leaned against the counter, admiring lyrics crafted by a gravy-bread-making lyricist. I yearned to catch her creative spark as she wrote "But Not Without You," undistracted by children and dogs racing in and out the kitchen door. "I like the taste of wine / And Auld Lang Syne / The shade of pine and a love all mine / But not without you. / I like a trip well planned / The feel of sand / A Dixieland band and Peter Pan / But not without you." I knew my mother in a new way. She had dreams, a calling, unsung skill. I scanned professionally-done sheet music for two 1957 originals, lyrics by J. McCarty with music by K. Marsh. Did I know K. Marsh? Did "I'm Goin' Home to Cry" and "Hello Spring" make it to the recording studio? Did June hear either tune performed, thrill to her words set to music? Hah, maybe I'll produce a recording of this double-sided gem. At the notion of bragging about her songs, I laughed way out loud.

"I wrote it," June often stated matter-of-factly when listening to certain songs, most especially Kitty Kallen's rendition of "Little Things Mean a Lot." I had no reason to question the songwriter. Indeed, I believed it for decades. What a night to recall. At a dinner party abuzz with hearty conversation, a guest casually asked June about her songwriting career. June looked puzzled. "Nobody knew you wrote 'Little Things Mean a Lot' until Marietta's talk," the blabbermouth continued. Properly astonished by the culprit's gullibility,

June cocked her head my way. Table talk stopped. Reality washed over me, forty-two years too late. "Why did you think I wrote that song, Marietta—it's by Richmond's own Carl Stutz and Edith Lindeman?" She waved away my mumbled reminder of her frequent claims. Her fingernails tapped out a theatrical tabletop drum roll. "I've also said that I met George Peppard for breakfast at Tiffany's. And, let's not forget, I was Puccini's favorite Madame Butterfly." Wine glasses refilled and grins broadened all but my face. "So, what else don't I know I've done, Marietta?" Eight of ten diners roared, mother and daughter united in mutual disbelief.

Cheered by the memory, I reopened the datebook to my innocent "Cole Porter" inscription—she'd implicated literal-minded me in her pretend piracy at an impressionable age. Flipping through the pages for more bounty, I came upon a letter from Plum to June, postmarked the summer after my college graduation. "I still think you gave up on this talent too soon," Plum praised. She had enclosed June's song "It's Never Too Late." A rush of love hit me. Another gut punch ended my search party. Her song called "I Saw a Rainbow Last Night" was folded over twice, the crease sealed by the songwriter's unmistakable lipstick smooch.

I put June's drawer back as she'd left it. Did she harbor any regrets about her curtailed career or was the pleasure of songwriting enough? Would she have liked to revisit the songs with me? Though I hadn't furthered the job of home emptying, it was days like this one that grounded and elevated me for three months. I'd filled up on memories of soul food and newfound soul music, staying put in the room that would be the hardest to leave for the last time.

But tomorrow, I had a bowl to fill. I failed miserably in a few halfhearted attempts to make June's potato salad. I'd written down the simple ingredients years ago and, foolishly confident, hadn't asked her for directions. Its secret lay there, in the step-by-step doing. I set out the ingredients for tomorrow's job, all pulled from pantry and cupboard—Yukon gold potatoes, olive oil, cider vinegar, Duke's mayonnaise, yellow onion, salt and pepper. My only instructions written from June's dictation lacked key information, but swaddled in early morning kitchen calm, maybe I'd fall naturally into my mother's way. "Mix well. Slice. Pour."

A new day, an old neighborhood dog walk, and my reenactment commenced. As boiled taters cooled, I chilled. Retracing old moves came easily—memory soon took over the job. In our largest measuring cup with a big spout, I "mixed well" the specified amounts of oil, vinegar, chopped onion, and mayo. Billy seemed to know the drill, walking in step with me from pantry to sink. Relaxing, I grew more confident with his validation. Salt and pepper left to my discretion, June's advice about all cooking suited me fine. "Put spice in a little at a time because you can add more but you can't take it out." I gently pulled off the skin from each potato, June-style, and "sliced," thin, but not too thin. It's here, in each precise move, oh yes 'tis. Picturing June at the counter, I saw one hand "pouring" and the other using a wide spoon for patting down potatoes. That's it— that's all. I placed a first layer of potato slices on the bottom of the bowl and imitated her slow pour and pat. Add another tater layer, pour and pat, repeat till done. How incredible, the surfacing of this long-internalized moment by moment memory. Refrigerate. Test tonight.

I'm catching on. The house potato salad required time and attention much like our meals that set the stage for amiable conversation. Shortcuts ruined my earlier potato salad efforts—mixing ingredients neither thoroughly nor often, using a peeler that mashed potatoes, ignoring layering for one big potato dump and pour-all. Home cooking isn't fast food. And communion demands and deserves our time.

Was the proof in my pudding? Matthew's son Harrison was stopping by to take some of "June's potato salad" to ailing Roger. Both cheeks bulging with potato salad pouches, Harrison's face wore the stamp of approval. I borrowed his testing ladle. It tasted just the same. "Tell me about this potato salad," he garbled. We sat down at the kitchen table.

Home cooking and the taste of good times, almost like the old days. And, I had plenty left for home-emptying helpers to enjoy tomorrow.

Cleaning up the kitchen, I looked over the sink into the backyard. The last two lines of the lipstick song rang true. The songwriter had scratched out her original last line after the phrase "I never thought it would happen." June penciled in her preferred ending.

"Oh, what a beautiful ride."

That Huge Desk in the Basement

I looked forward to a quiet day at 1203—a slowdown to reflect, assess my home-emptying progress, complete a few chores, and hatch a plan forward. Certain that I could never be "alone" in the two rooms where I'd spend most of the day, I hit "play" on an hour-length home movie during the drive to Richmond. The basement stole the show.

Overjoyed at the news that 1203 was officially ours, the four of us skedaddled from our Keswick Gardens third-floor apartment to stake our claim. For months we'd scoped out houses under adult consideration for our first home, and at long last we'd explore the one we all loved at every sighting. Oh, golly, that first glimpse of the castle on a hill. Accompanied by the music of our heels clacking on pine floors, we flung open doors and closets, this child's imagination in flight. Three floors, three bedrooms, a separate living room and dining room, both a porch and a den, front and back yards, and a garage—was this a dream? But the room that I remembered best from that thrilling day revealed itself last. At our fastest clip, Patrick and I pounded down twelve squeaky steps from the kitchen to the basement and jogged around its vast perimeter like Olympic athletes circling a stadium. An indoor playground! We yelled, "It's a wonderland," over and over, egged on by the echo of our voices reverberating from cinderblock walls and tile floor, two kids struck silly by our good fortune.

My father slowed his children's pace going down this stair-case, his measured stride, always the same, the metronome of my childhood. This getaway space, burrowed underground, would become his sanctuary and, for me, the place for one-of-a-kind happenings. His niece and nephews, neighborhood kids, actually any child who knew better beat feet down those creaky steps to hang out with the kind man who loved them. Even items long-removed from the basement retain its distinct, indelible smell—a mixture of pipe tobacco, musty books, the oil furnace, shoe polish, mothballs, bleach, and laundry detergent.

Beginning with trips home from college and ending only with my purposely-delayed ownership of a washer and dryer, upon arrival I tossed a duffle bag jammed with dirty laundry from the top of the basement steps to the floor. Hearing the familiar thud, Mac responded with a peppy invitation to "Come on down, Baby." We picked up wherever we hadn't left off, two fast friends at home in their basement cocoon.

That thud would resound on this laundry day at 1203. Dirties had been mounting with visits from friends and family. Pillowcases plumped with sheets, sheets tied in bows stuffed with bath towels, bath towels wrapped around hand and dish towels—a parade soon sailing down the basement steps for an old father-daughter activity. I looked forward to the old routine. Wash, dry, fold, laundry up. Relax. Wash, dry, fold, laundry up. Relax.

Basement reverie ended along with my travel mug of coffee when I slowed at the sign for our exit. Billy's head popped up as he sniffed the scents that escorted us the short ride home. We lazed in the backyard, one of us watering plants and the other chasing squirrels. Leaving Billy in charge upstairs, I inhaled the unique perfume the moment I opened the basement door. Laundry down—fire in the hole!

By now much of the basement had been packed up and cleared out. I descended, instead, to the basement of my childhood.

Shoes, tools, dust rags, and baskets lined the steps on each side, waiting in line to go upstairs or down, sooner or likely later. Hats and coats layered on pegs along the stairwell and collages of photographs covered its walls. I paid attention to each unique creak, three steps showing signs of sagging middles, and landed at the bottom amidst today's pile of laundry. Taking a right at the bottom of the stairs with bundles in both hands, I entered the dimly-lit "Furnace Room." Radiating warmth for the basement, the serious-looking oil container's rumble guaranteed household heat and hot water. The faithful washer and dryer stood side by side near the double sink—a hose dumped water from washing machine to sink, and a dryer vent poked outside through a small ground-level window. My first of many loads of laundry churning, I took note of my surroundings.

Another small window over the sink provided enough light for a Christmas cactus and a winding philodendron. Two clotheslines stretched the room, end to end. Clothespins, detergent, bleach, and stain remover claimed regular spots on the laundry-folding table. Paint cans and brushes, a toolbox, many-sized and multipurpose Mason jars galore, Christmas decorations and wrapping paper, tubes of glue and lubricating oil, baskets hanging from hooks in the rafters—an accidental curiosity shop. Strategically placed flashlights illuminated dark corners and shed light on overhead mysteries. Big clothes bags fastened by zippers hung from rods. Seldom-used power tools, probably gifts, gathered dust together. Boxes of books packed for safekeeping, some labeled by owner and others by genre, served as the 1203 giveaway library.

My father fashioned a section of this toasty area for his "dressing room." After showering upstairs, clad in terrycloth robe he headed to the basement to dress for the day. Suits dangled on hangers from an improvised clothes rack, an ironed white handkerchief with precise, crisp points already in place in each jacket pocket. Bermuda shorts and colorful casual shirts contrasted with workday belts, cufflinks, starched shirts, and ties. Mac's shoes, arranged in his methodical way, took on personalities—wingtips that laced up for banker's hours, black high tops and white tennis shoes for play, galoshes and boots for outdoor duties, and brown and black loafers (maybe sporting a penny in the slit on top) for a good time, any time. My favorites danced in his college days, two-tone black and white size thirteens, black leather base and soft white tops, three rows of thin, black laces tying up these special-occasion party shoes. They waited, always polished, next to his shoeshine kit, a wooden box with a foot-shaped top for buffing and open sides stocked with polishes, rags, and brushes.

I crossed through one of the two openings on either end of the furnace room into the other side of the basement. I choked back tears standing in the unkempt room anchored by a huge oak desk, a matching swivel rocker fitting snugly under its center. Carried by four movers down the outdoor steps and barely squeezing through an unhinged basement door, this one piece of furniture grounded the house. It moved not a whit. Fittingly it would be the last object to leave 1203.

Deep drawers left and right of the chair in the middle, warping over time and requiring jiggling, contained labeled file folders, manila envelopes, onion-skin paper, treasured letters and cards, stationery, grade school report cards, check books and registers, and bills marked *paid*. A shallow drawer ran across the desk's width above the chair, its indented front lip brimming with rubber bands, paper clips, staples, pens and pencils, Luden's gummy throat lozenges, spearmint lifesavers, multi-colored packs of chewing gum called "chiclets" (green and white my preference), and pipe cleaners. The spacious desktop had room for a big lamp, reading glasses, rulers, an adding machine used also by children imitating a banker at work, a globe, and an Underwood typewriter with its round and thick, black and white keys. A ground level window beamed sunlight over the desk. The nearby dehumidifier provided a readymade stool for a child. Shelves ringed the room, more boxes of books and magazines lined the floor (piles of "Archie Comics" featuring my pal Jughead), and a couple of folding chairs stood at-the-ready for sidling up to the desk. Next to a thick dictionary, several copies of the same edition of the newspaper lay on the desktop's right corner, every week a six-inch stack.

The afternoon paper, the *Richmond News Leader,* challenged readers with its weekly crossword puzzle nicknamed "Cashwords," which my father played to win every week. I fumbled through the shallow top drawer for an old clipping, and sure enough found a neatly-folded newspaper article dated February 21, 1964. Mac the mathematician usually hedged his bet, submitting more than one set of puzzle answers after calculating the odds. But in the article toasting his victory prize (out of 18,800 entries!) of $375.00, he admitted that he almost forgot that week and dashed off his one submission, mailing it with a snap of his fingers for luck. "I always feel lucky until I read that someone else won." Accurately described by the reporter as a "tall, good-natured executive with an easy style," Mr. McCarty's photograph pictures him handing over the winning check to a teller at his bank. "The best thing to do is put it in a savings account and not spend it. If it had come a little earlier, I could've told you what I would do with it. I had a wedding anniversary on February 7."

A constant presence, I see him bent over that week's crossword, occasionally humming off-key or whistling softly, and somehow keeping his concentration as we amused ourselves—honing our skills in cat-quick games of pick-up sticks, snatching metal jack rocks before the second bounce of the rubber ball, or playing more sedentary contests of Parcheesi, rarely-completed Monopoly, checkers, or cards. Patrick erected a Lincoln Log fort, populating his tiny town with imaginary sidekicks Biggie, Kiki, and Joey. I read not-for-school books. Simple games, nothing fancy, we feasted on undemanding, leisure-assuring pleasures.

Mac positioned a small black and white television on a stand for occasional viewing from his desk. His tears fell when the four of us gathered around the desk for the funeral of President Kennedy. Mac and I watched Dizzy Dean and Pee Wee Reese as the former ballplayers broadcast Saturday's Major League Game of the Week. I longed to spend time in the booth with this goofy duo. We tried to solve murders before "Perry Mason" fingered the criminal, searched for clues with Perry's cool, suave private investigator Paul Drake, and presumed secretary Della Street knew more than she let on. We cranked up the volume on one Ed Sullivan Show, trying to hear The Beatles tell me "I Want to Hold Your Hand" over the cries of a berserk audience. I looked for any excuse to retreat underground, cagily choosing a chore that promised me even more quality basement time—the ironing board, iron, sprinkling can, and bin of wrinkled clothes all stationed right next to that big desk. After school, I ironed while twisting with dancers on "American Bandstand," questioning even then why Dick Clark never aged. I wedged in line with older kids stepping to "The Stroll," and, not for lack of effort, admitted that my version of "The Shimmy" would have to wait.

I sat on the bottom step and savored basement yesterdays. Its coziness still proved irresistible. I was startled by the sound of my voice on the phone in the emptying room—my words, echoing off cinderblock and tile, so like the hollow sounds of two ecstatic kids screaming during their first laps around their gigantic new base-ment. My heart swelled with tender, aching emotion that only my father's basement could have evoked.

Yes, important things happened when I slid into a chair be-side his oak desk. I watched and then helped Mac cover my text-books with thick brown paper that would protect them until their return at the end of the school year, a hands-on lesson on the value of a book. He let me pick from the thirteen gilt-edged, pocketsize volumes of the *Complete Works of William Shakespeare,* organized chronologically in a rectangular flip top box bound by red gros-grain ribbon—I stared in disbelief at a barely discernable 1857 date on the bottom of the box, even more astonished by the writer's cockamamie English. My dad helped me with math like a Zen Mas-ter—listening to mindless recitation of memorized "Times Tables," returning my sulking glare at a long division problem with a smile, patiently climbing the impenetrable wall I erected for protection from subtracting fractions. He quizzed me on the meaning of new "vocabulary," both of us laughing when he tossed in an impossible word that wasn't on my list, and thereby taught me the definitions of "esoteric" or "behemoth." ("Use the word in a sentence. Okay, our station wagon is a behemoth.") I learned to balance my first check-book and the rationale for making regular deposits in a savings ac-count while leaning on a small shelf that, with a tug at its indenta-tions, shimmied out into a miniature desk.

Most significantly, my father and I talked about things that I was sure no one else did—the passage of time, selflessness, sorrow, generosity, peace, humility. He invited me into comfortable silence. I felt smart with him. When we asked each other a question, often the question itself satisfied us. I thrived on this wordless communi-cation, both of us thinking our own thoughts together. The after-glow of these conversations burns bright.

Mac lasered in on one topic in particular. His insistence that rudeness was inexcusable, always, every single time, lodged in my heart. Why did he target rudeness, I wondered, but not for long. Our dialogue wafted between us with ease, nudging us ever closer to a satisfying understanding. How does rudeness differ from anger? He and I traded ideas, offered abstract examples of rude behavior, described how it would make the recipient feel. Then, quietly, my pop told me of times that he'd been treated rudely—and even at age ten, I shared unfortunate experiences for the first time. Searching for the motivation of a rude act, we arrived at an ugly conclusion. All of our examples of rudeness, imagined and real, had one characteristic in common. Rudeness is intentional—a premeditated choice to dismiss or embarrass. Neither forced nor uncontrollable, rude behavior is absolutely unnecessary.

He never backed off. How well I recall Mac's awkward foot-shuffling at my college graduation when he first thought that I was ignoring the person standing next to him. Dad! I didn't speak to her by name because I don't know her. His face melted with relief.

Six loads of laundry behind me, I fetched balls with Billy in the backyard. He'd tired of my subterranean absence, the basement the only bit of 1203 unknown to him. Legs too short, steps too steep, one bumpy ride enough basement exposure for this smart guy. I carried him down.

He looked to me for guidance—a milestone.

Propelling myself in the swivel chair around the newly roomy basement, a grown-up child at heart, I pulled under center at the desk. Billy stretched out beside the chair, another kid drawn to the oak mystique. Pulling out a legal pad and sharp pencil, I made two lists. One, a written to-do list, matched tasks with helpers for the upcoming weekend's workdays. The other, a mental list for my lifetime reference:

Boo to you, foolish rudeness. Check.

Arrogance begone, bragging so gross. Check.

Generosity and humility go hand in hand. Check.

Choose words carefully—often, go wordless. Check.

My last conversation with my sensitive and wise dad passed between us silently. We'd always been two trusting basement philosophers, chatting, listening, joking, prepping for life.

Clean the dryer vent. Check.

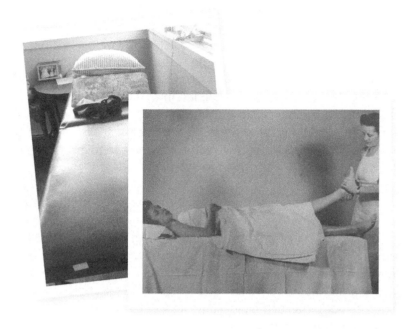

A Massage Table, an Insurance Policy, and Short Stories

Plum's presence was everywhere from the start at 1203. Her nimble fingers—always with manicured and painted nails—snapped string beans, braided rugs and my pigtails, needlepointed pillows and chairs. Her hands passed trays of her signature Smithfield ham biscuits, served platters of piping hot crab cakes, and gently cupped gardenia blossoms and children's faces. Her six grandchildren returned spanking clean plates for seconds of her peach cobbler, cherry and apples pies, and coconut string cake. She came alive today, waiting for me inside an envelope in her dresser, behind a picture frame, and within a dust-covered wood box.

Plum's antique dresser, its drawers stuffed with everyday wear and a stash of keepsakes, centered her bedroom wherever she lived. Running my hand over the top of the dresser this morning, I thought of another home emptying in 1996 and the dresser's eventual placement that day under her mirror here in my childhood bedroom. Her eyes remained downcast as my friends carried the dresser out of her apartment—she was moving in with June, parting with twenty-five years of memories and her independence. My grandmother sat in the only chair left in an empty living room, legs crossed, purse in her lap, unmoving. Standing in the doorway, waiting for her, I couldn't fully appreciate then her unshakeable sense of loss. We rode together in silence, the moving van following my car home to 1203 only a few miles away.

I lifted the bottom drawer of the dresser onto the bed for closer inspection. As I'd hoped, this drawer was a catchall of mementos, nary a handkerchief or scarf spoiling the fun. Photographs aplenty ranged from her 1904 baby picture to her ninety-fifth birthday festivities on the patio. A century passed before my eyes. Look at my grandmother the sixth-grader, standing tall shortly after her adored mother died, the oldest in a row of five children. Plum's formal education ended when she assumed the role of her siblings' surrogate parent during their father's work-related absences. Now a young woman, she shucks corn and shells lima beans, floats downriver on an inner tube, strums her ukulele for a singalong. Plum at sixty-two zooms off on the motor scooter she's given grandson Daniel for his birthday. Our picnicking octogenarian grandmother, kerchiefed head thrown back in pure delight and sundress hiked high, perches on rocks amidst rushing water in Goshen Pass. Ninety-three-year-old Plum the country girl bottle-feeds a baby goat before blowing out the candles on her cake, all decked out in a brocade jacket and wool skirt. She models red, medium-high heels in her favorite style, one of four pairs in different colors she purchased after her hospital stay ten years earlier.

What a free-for-all collection in the drawer just for me, featuring random potpourri pouches, Mardi Gras beads, filled passports, maps of Cape Cod and Copenhagen, a senior pass to National Parks, and clip-on sunglasses. I placed two items next to the lamp on the dresser—these finds brought a chuckle on the spot and guaranteed a cheery finish to the day. Near the bottom of this Pandora's box, one large envelope lay flat, sandwiched between folders of postcards and letters. I opened the intriguing packet stamped by Dementi Studio.

Look at those gals. I'd heard the stories and now stared at picture-perfect evidence. A series of striking eight by ten, black and white photographs showcased my grandmother the masseuse, the choreographed sequence surely intended to promote her career. A woman in her late teens lay on her mother's massage table, June's eyes closed with her head cradled in a pillow, one crisp sheet beneath her and one on top. Plum's attire consisted of a long white skirt with high waist and a modest white halter top that wrapped around the back and tied in a loose knot at her neck. Her poses foreshadowed the precise movements of massage therapists today. She leaned her elbow into pressure points, her unmistakable hands kneaded tight shoulders and released tension in necks and hamstrings. The vibrant masseuse exuded strength, her sleeveless garb revealed toned biceps, and her big wristwatch assured faithful adherence to a packed schedule.

What a "to do" list she must have checked off each day. Has there ever been a more resourceful person than this single mother of two girls, June born in 1923, EJ in 1925? Little did I know when first studying the pre-and-post Depression period that someone so dear to me experienced firsthand the fear and deprivation of those years—especially my fun-loving, daredevilish grandmother. On the day she moved to 1203, two men struggled to carry her massage table to the basement, the table that she hoisted up three and four flights of stairs to her clients' apartments. Tracing Plum's journey, I revisited the Depression years, up close.

When I reached again into the envelope, I discovered more tools of her trade. Though she was born Nellie Eliza Williamson, her official, monogrammed stationery read Hilda Swensen. Her specialty was highlighted on the bill that she presented to her clients

"For Professional Services" rendered by "Miss Swensen," Richmond's expert in Swedish massage! As a child, I never questioned the back-and-forth switches, a cousin calling her Nellie and her second husband introducing her to his friends as Hilda. After all, she also answered to my first attempts to call out to her from my crib. "Plum! Plum!" I beseeched her, imitating her nickname for me, "Sugar Plum," as best I could. She was "Plum" for life to one and all, and she crowned me Prissy Prune, PP for short. I learned of her ingenious workaday pseudonym when Plum regaled my college friends (and me) with tales of her "Swedish" years.

Next, I pulled a pamphlet from the illuminating envelope, a handout for her clients entitled "Health and Beauty through Diet and Massage." I considered some excerpts. "On arising, drink the juice of a half lemon in a glass of warm water. Don't start thinking about dinner until you sit down to eat it as mental pictures of food make you twice as hungry. Don't sit still after a meal, especially dinner. Get up and walk, dance, or work. Let the last thing you do before jumping into bed be a good fifteen or twenty minutes of exercise (I will gladly show you the exercises)." Yes, she would. But my oh my, what a fibber: "Knowing how we Southerners like vegetables cooked with ham, bacon, or salt pork, I can only say: Beware!" I can taste her delicious, salty untruths. How satisfying it must have been for her to receive testimony from clients and their families, such heartfelt gratitude expressed in their well-preserved letters to "our dearest Hilda"—many a thank you for restoring health and instilling hope, lessening arthritis pain, rekindling joy in physical activity.

I held the empty envelope, imagining. My mother marveled in retrospect, as I did now, that she and EJ never wanted for anything. Each morning after a hot breakfast, the sisters walked from their home to nearby Westhampton School—best friends clad in crisply-ironed dresses and patent leather shoes, bookbags strapped on shoulders and lunchboxes full of goodies swinging at their sides. Every Christmas Eve a fresh, decorated tree appeared, beautifully wrapped presents enticingly arranged beneath the lowest branches. Photograph albums testify to merry Christmases and happy birthdays, detailed records of abiding joy despite hard times. What better teacher of the value of disciplined work, of putting one dogged foot in front of another, of simply doing what needs to be done?

Plum's legendary stamina stayed with her until the end, and she transformed the forced frugality of those lean years into culinary art. She created delicious soup from the tough stalks of asparagus spears. Supper leftovers morphed into gourmet lunches. Hot meals were served on hot plates, always, no exception. Paper towels dried over counter edges. Plum cracked open the oven door during winter months, heating nearby rooms while her buttermilk biscuits cooled on the kitchen table. She transmitted her lessons in frugality by example—living well and within modest means seems natural and right to me. And no one relished the occasional splurge more than thrifty Plum—she earned it. She shared it. Thrift afforded the means for her lifetime of unstinting generosity.

Trying not to think about eating beforehand lest it make me ravenous, I enjoyed a leisurely lunch in the den. Surveying the status of home-emptying progress in this room, I noticed a slightly crooked picture frame, its backing visible in a bottom corner. Straightening the picture, I felt thick, stiff parchment on the back. Upon examination, I found a familiar document that June must have taped, and then forgotten, behind a photograph of her mother.

I re-read this history lesson, recalling my first sighting of life insurance policy #MI508541, dated July 27, 1931. Serving as Plum's executor in 2000, I drove to the bank one last time before closing the books. Had I missed anything? I opened the lockbox Plum shared with June, and for the first time noticed a yellowing, tattered envelope amidst June's papers. Inside hid the fanciest, oldest official document I'd ever seen—proof of life insurance purchased by Plum for "eleven cents" per month. She named her beloved younger sister Jennie, who often cared for Plum's daughters while the masseuse worked, the beneficiary. In 1951, she made grownup June, mother of two babies, sole beneficiary.

When I "redeemed" Plum's policy, those multiples of eleven cents starting in 1931 totaled $4500.00 in 2000. Even the Prudential agent rejoiced in our gift from Plum, returning the original policy to June for framing. She and I searched futilely for years for this document that was framed already in its secretive way.

Today, I had intended a room-by-room house check, but halfway done, I decided to spend the rest of this day with Plum. Thinking back on her moving day to 1203, I knew at once where to hunt for more of her. Flashlight in hand, I fast walked impatiently to the basement. The movers had stacked boxes marked "basement" in a section that I'd cleared for storing Plum's things—items she couldn't part with but probably wouldn't revisit. I shone the light against the back wall of the utility room beside the furnace. Plum's storage area looked at first sight just as the movers had left it, untouched and forgotten. I poked around mounds of boxes, dark masking tape curling but still securing their sagging cardboard lids. I sifted through canning jars and a pressure cooker, metal file drawers with labeled color slides and a projector. Round hatboxes in mint condition looked as stylish as the hats within. Holding the beam steady on an unfamiliar, handcrafted, knot-holed box, I couldn't resist. Twisting it free from its surroundings, I carried it upstairs into the den. Billy jumped down from the footstool in front of June's wingchair and I sat with the dusty box in front of me.

Land Sakes Alive! A batch of short stories penned in the late nineteen-twenties and thirties, authored by Nell Williamson and her ghost writer Hilda Swensen.

When I took my first small steps into a possible writing career, my mother mentioned casually, from time to time, that "your grandmother was a writer, too, and she sent a number of short stories to publishing houses." The whereabouts of her stories unknown, Plum as writer receded from my memory. The old pine and oak box was just the right size for my father's meticulously organized folders, one for each of the almost thirty stories. Plum the rookie typist two-fingered longer pieces while she penned others in dark blue India ink using her prized Parker fountain pen. "Vacation for Two," "Smitten," "Sand in Her Shoes," "Upstream" (note, 57,181 words), "Clicking," "Grandpa's Moment." Rusting paperclips bound shorter tales. Through her stories, I met a girl not yet my grandmother. How did she summon the late-night energy? What stoked her imagination? When did my father become her manager?

Oh, how close the masseuse-by-day came to publication. Encouraging editor's notes from G. Glenwood Clark filled the margins of certain stories. A ripped-open, empty envelope from Macfadden Publications, 1926 Broadway, New York must have thrilled her upon its arrival. I read from "Sand in Her Shoes," amazed. "Empty lobster claws rattling on plates, ladies trying to out talk their male companions, and soft music from the radio became events sharply pronounced against the continued roar of the ocean." And a page later, "As the water rolled between her and home she got her first real conception of the size and greatness of the earth."

Lacking her discipline, I turned to the beginning of "Upstream," her longest. "Nestling peacefully amongst the New England hills, remote from all traffic activity, sits a small rambling cottage. In this beautiful yet simple little home, on the very morning of which I am starting my story, live seven people who by a twist of fate created the most fable-like story that I've ever read, much less had the joy and sorrow of living." And on page six: "I went to the window, raised the shade, and watched as she made her way carefully down the steps. She pulled her coat closely around her, then stopped and looked around to see if anyone was watching. Assuring herself they weren't, she slipped her foot out of a shoe, folded her handkerchief into a little square and placed it in her shoe. That picture stayed in my mind for years."

I yearned for her to have seen her words in print. "Oh, spit!" as she would say when dealt a bad hand in canasta or when the top on her pressure cooker blew.

Plum endured another disappointment during this time. A studio portrait of very pretty twenty-six-year-old Plum protruded above the horizontal folders, protected by matte backing and supported by the back of the box. A slight smile graces her soft, pensive face. Thick hair falls in waves around her shoulders, unlike the workaday look of her dark brown hair pulled back by barrettes. In slightly-smudged ink at the bottom left an inscription reads: "May I always be your sweet-heart? To Jimmy from Nell. November 8, 1930." Jimmy? Yes, I recall June and EJ talking together about a trumpeter in Richmond's most popular big band—a good-looking fellow named Jimmy, remembered by her daughters as the love of Plum's life. They guessed that her beau backed away from the courtship because the deal included two little girls whom he correctly anticipated would always come first. Plum, as usual, walked on with her trademark quick steps.

After a day of keeping pace with my intrepid grandmother, I was exhausted and completely lost in her world. Billy walked me around the neighborhood and returned me home. I retrieved those two rewards, purposely set aside this morning, from the top of Plum's dresser—sheet music and a spiral notepad.

"Skylark," the song I played in my first piano recital, still bore the teacher's boldly punctuated comments. Sister Patricia had figured out that I had memorized the movement of her hands rather than learned to "read" the notes. I practiced scales on a "Winter Musette," this spectacular piano a surprise in 1958 from Plum. She came to visit from Florida months after its delivery, and we sat together on the piano bench for which she had needlepointed a cushiony cover. I performed my go-to tune, "Surrey with the Fringe on Top," confidently striking that one repetitive note that insisted "chicks and ducks and geese better scurry." She was properly pleased. I never wondered how Plum afforded a piano.

Today I laughed aloud at her clever feat, gleefully recalling that early morning confession. Lying in my bed upstairs, too excited to sleep on Plum's arrival days, I loved hearing the happy commotion when already-talking Plum burst through the kitchen door. June and Mac waited for her with a sunrise breakfast. This particular homecoming topped them all. The trio spoke all at once, interrupting and repeating phrases for emphasis, their laughter raucous. I had to concentrate on every word, holding my breath, to get the scoop on the piano's purchase. Wide-eyed, I solved the mystery. Jesse, Plum's husband, budgeted all household expenses, so she shopped for groceries with a pre-set weekly food allowance. After dining for months on Plum's repertoire of ground beef specialties—sloppy joe's, meatloaf, stuffed bell peppers, meatballs (Swedish), and hamburgers with grilled onions—Jesse looked up from his plate at the dinner table. "Hilda, are we ever going to eat steak again?" Hysteria broke out in the 1203 kitchen. "Let me see that piano!" the frugal chef roared. Pennies saved, a piano earned.

Now, for the second gem. Each page of the flip notepad served as scorecard for a game of Scrabble. Plum's name topped a slanting column on one side and her opponent's the other, the careful running tally building in suspense. She took on all comers—Mac her favorite and best challenger—and won almost every contest. She conceded defeat rarely and only after consulting a dictionary to verify the spelling of any suspicious words. Plum, the wordsmith at eighty-two, visited my college philosophy class to unrestrained student delight. She sat attentively, straight-backed and hands folded, always learning. Days later she called with a question about class. "I don't know what 'isness' means. I hoped one of your students would ask. Did you make it up?" She was in a hurry. "It's okay, PP. Loved your class, Darling. I just don't want to play isness on the board tonight and get penalized if it's not a word."

She doted on me, her first grandchild, beyond reason and measure. Today I doted on my chock-full-of-gumption-and-generosity grandmother right back.

Three Baseball Bats and a Tennis Racquet

1203 closets run deep and wide. Lacking lighting, their recesses and cubbies make excellent hiding places. I had great expectations for the one closet most likely to retain the prizes of my youth.

During our first week residing at 1203, I laid claim to my assigned bedroom, so big and mine alone. Deliberately placing items in the closet, one by slow one, I hung school uniforms at the front of the clothes rack, play and party clothes behind these official blazers and skirts, and coats at the rear. The hanging clothes formed a screen for hideaway items in the roomy space extending behind the rack. Here I stashed shoeboxes of baseball cards arranged by teams, baseballs and gloves, an empty scrapbook, and a transistor radio for late night. Dropping school saddle shoes on the floor along with my navy blue Keds with holes poking through canvas toes, I hooked resoled penny loafers and dressy flats on the built-in shoe rack.

Recommitting the original, perfect closet to memory, I tugged open the old door, sticky with age and humidity. The knob fit just right in my hand. My once tidy private space served now as a storage chamber. I pulled one thing after another off the clothes rack, mostly Plum's, making room for further investigation. Seeking a path to old pay dirt, the hunt was on. The clothes rack cleared at last, I peered into the dark recesses behind it, aided by an old flashlight with a dim, flickering light.

The morning's project braked to a joyous full stop. I struck gold.

My three baseball bats stood upright in a crevice at the far back of the closet, safe from prying hands back then and almost my own today. Ducking low, I brought out each precious bat one at a time. Play ball! I twirled my first, shorter than regulation, dark brown bat, delighting in the familiar feel of electrical tape wound around the handle. Surely my father's solution, the tape provided a secure grip for a small-handed batter and safety for the pitcher. I swung, connecting for a standup double, and leaned the bat under the sill of a small window across from the closet. Batter up! I recognized the bulk of my long, gray "Hanna" model, so heavy that it swung me as a child, challenging me anew as I lugged it to the makeshift bat rack under the window sill. Out came my pale-yellow Louisville Slugger, which I planned on taking to the Major Leagues. Grand Slam! The three bats resting side by side, I crossed my fingers for more sports treasure and shook the flashlight awake.

Billy, cooling on the pine floor, slept through a loud shout when further rummaging revealed my Sam B. Woods autographed Bancroft tennis racquet, locked by four screws in a metal press to prevent warping. A squishy white tennis ball, identified as a Pennsylvania #2, was jammed in a nearby corner. I stretched my back, stiff from closet sleuthing, swinging the racquet now freed from its press—a couple of forehands and backhands, punched volleys, an abbreviated overhead. How beautiful, my worn, sweat-stained grip. I lined up the racquet, a gift from its namesake, alongside the bats and pulled a rocker up to the window. All my childhood, I had gazed through this small porthole down the tree-lined street into the big world. Today I'd rock and remember.

Countless twists and turns mark the course of any life—the defining moments grasped only in retrospect. Looking back from the perspective of my old bedroom, I know for sure that the ability to play tennis changed my life. The dilapidated tennis ball in the palm of my hand was a souvenir from my first Richmond City Championship win. The path to that victory began one miserable day as I sat on my father's knee. It fell to my dad to break the crushing news to me.

Enjoying our special retreat at his desk in the basement, I didn't see it coming. Mac cleared his throat and addressed me in a shaky voice. "Sweetie, you'll find other games you love, but you won't grow up and play second base at Yankee Stadium. You can't—girls play softball, not baseball." A "soft" ball? What in the world? I understood the tears in the eyes of the nicest man in the world. He was lying! Mac the mean! Somebody put him up to this trick. Was his pronouncement connected to my grandmother's gift of a tennis racquet and a can of balls? Get me to the nearest dugout.

Thus far I've mapped out a career plan only once—as an eight-year-old beribboned, pigtailed ballplayer. At the beginning of my distinguished professional career, I'd live at home and play for the Richmond Virginians, the Yankees Minor League farm club, developing skills until my manager summoned me to his office to say that I was going to the "Show," the Big Leagues. Spectators filed into Yankee Stadium. From box seats and bleachers, they pointed to me fielding grounders at second base, batting eighth, a regular in the lineup, and a fan favorite despite a weak batting average. My specialties included distracting base runners, laying down sacrifice bunts, and jogging to the mound to calm the pitcher's nerves.

I was (am) wild about this game. We all loved baseball—listening to games on the radio, reading aloud the box scores in the morning newspaper, wagering a nickel on World Series games in pools running at Big Daddy's market, Mac's bank, and at school if we could get away with it. Happy were the Sundays that my father dropped my grandfather and me at Parker Field where we spent the afternoon taking in a doubleheader. Big Daddy spoiled me with a bat or three, mitt, and hardballs, everything I needed for neighborhood pickup games. He had Wednesday afternoons off from his job at the market. Waiting with June for his Westhampton #16 bus to circle to its stop near the University of Richmond, I planned our baseball practice.

My mother knew her baseball, second-guessing Casey Stengel and correctly anticipating pinch hitters, appreciating the outfield's green spaciousness and the batter's nerves as he waited in the on-deck circle. She purchased priceless living room seats for us to watch afternoon World Series games—I played hooky with parental insistence. We debated the merits of Dodger centerfielder Duke Snider and his Yankee counterpart Mickey Mantle. What a swell vacation—eating popcorn, standing for the seventh inning stretch, rooting for the underdog. Darn. Having been recruited to play a new game, I'd soon play the underdog role.

Reluctant at the outset, I rode with my forgiven father to the tennis courts on nearby school playgrounds and in public parks. I hit balls against the backboard at Westhampton School until the backboard conceded. Big Daddy continued to sneak me a baseball wrapped in butcher's paper, but this other game with its odd scorekeeping was okay. I dazzled myself in my white Converse tennis shoes, rubber tips at the toes. I admired them from all angles—soles, sides, shoelaces. I could hit a ball in tennis, too, maybe not as far as a baseball and with more restrictions, but I could hit more of them. I experienced the sweet surprise of the ball sailing from my racquet across the net, then coming back to me, and shockingly my racquet sending the ball back over again, and again. Mac often took me to play on the courts at Byrd Park where we indulged in grape and lime snow-cones after our "game." He tossed me ball after ball, standing perilously close to my swings, a beginner himself.

One fine day as we picked up balls scattered across three courts at Byrd Park, a man much older than my dad approached the chain link fence, doffed his straw hat after putting down a bucket of balls. "I've been watching your daughter hit the ball. Would you like me to give her some lessons?" he asked. He taught me, for free, and gave me a gift with a lifetime guarantee.

Sam B. Woods instructed three generations of Richmond kids in the art of playing the game to which he devoted his life. His teaching style was simple, direct: keep your eye on the ball, bend your knees (he must have wearied of that one), turn your side to the net. "Make the last one good," he challenged with a hard-to-get last ball in the bucket. He said little and I paid close attention. "I hope I live long enough to see Marietta get to Wimbledon," he confided to my dad. That dream of playing on England's famed grass courts commenced with my first tournament away from home at age ten, playing singles and doubles in the 12, 14, 16, and 18-and-under divisions in Suffolk, Virginia. So homesick that I should have been disqualified, calling home collect at 6am, I lost 6-0, 6-0 in all eight matches. When I returned to 1203 to hand over my racquet, my parents assured me that it was "great experience." Really? But I improved, playing locally, regionally, nationally, and at Hollins College. It was the game for me. The world opened up as I traveled to tournaments, treating me to new people, faraway places, and tough decision making. I passed along this terrific game, teaching lessons during college summers, graduate school, at the community college, and directing a summer tennis camp—earning income by playing ball, a slight alteration of my original scheme.

August 14, 1963 flashed across the screen of this home movie. I'd known it was coming, a replay of the most important albeit painful day of my lifetime in sports.

After a morning doubles match and lunch at 1203, June and I set out for my two o'clock finals match in the summer-ending invitational tournament at Byrd Park. I was both excited to play a newcomer to Richmond tournaments and also relieved that the unsettling week was coming to an end. All week long, I had sensed an undertow of tension at the courts, adults strangely quiet in carpools and while watching matches and tournament organizers anxious about the schedule of play. As for me, I had two concerns. First, I didn't know my opponent except by reputation—her winning record earned her the number one seed, my customary ranking. Who was this highly-touted Bonnie Logan, and why had I not encountered her before? And weighing more heavily on me, Mr. Woods wouldn't be at the Park today, hospitalized after a bad fall earlier in the week. Was he getting better?

As June and I turned onto The Boulevard, we saw parked cars lining the curbs on both sides of the wide medians, a string of vehicles many long blocks from the courts. I tightened my grip on the trusty Bancroft racquet. My mom confirmed in a gentle tone what my stomach understood as I observed the sidewalk parade—they were indeed arriving for my match. I'd never played before such a throng. I looked more closely, not recognizing many faces, though a number of walkers waved and wished me luck. I realized that skin color determined the makeup of every cluster of animated people walking toward the courts. Though I'd not seen this distinction at other tournaments, I didn't give it much thought.

At the courts, sports reporters jotted notes and interviewed other players, photographers clicked away—quite a hubbub. Three hundred people squeezed onto the bleachers.

Pockets of spectators scattered around the grassy area, stretched out on blankets and seated in strategically-placed lawn chairs. If only my teacher could see all this, I wished, as June and I passed by the court where he had introduced himself and offered to give me a few lessons. From afar my doubles partner hurried toward us, running against the flow going to the match. "Did you hear that Mr. Woods died this morning?" She walked away at a fast clip, probably embarrassed by my outpouring of tears. A reassuring hand firmly at my back, my mother walked forward with me.

I pulled most of me together and reported to the check-in table where I met Bonnie. She was friendly and shy and respected my obvious emotion. We walked side by side to Court One, met the umpire, and began our warm-ups. I spotted my father in the stands, decked out in his business suit and tie, having left the bank just in time for the 2pm match. Mr. Woods's pupils filled the entire front row of the bleachers, loyally and tearfully cheering me on.

Playing the best match of my life, I lost 6-4, 7-5. Big-time applause escalated as Bonnie and I shook hands at the net. This was as close as I got to "The Show," holding my own against a true talent. Seeking my dad again through misty eyes, I saw him reach across the black and white color barrier to offer a handshake or hug to those across the divide. Color-based segregation in the stands and all over the grounds gave way to back slaps and big laughs, a strangely exuberant ending to a tennis match.

I had competed in the first integrated match in a sanctioned tournament on the public courts in Richmond, a civil right denied to Richmond's legendary champion Arthur Ashe. The historical significance escaped me that day, though I sadly comprehended the rarity of this kind of communal gathering.

Shortly after our only meeting, Bonnie Logan's career sky-rocketed and she made her mark internationally. I rooted her on, a fan of the bravest girl in town on August 14, 1963. An article the next day in the *Richmond Times-Dispatch* detailed the size of the crowd, breaks of serve (twelve), my placement of two forehands to tie the first set 4-4, the seesawing score, and the length of our match (one hour and forty minutes)—everything but the reason for the large crowd. Two weeks later Martin Luther King, Jr. shared his dream with the world from the Lincoln Memorial.

I sat with the lessons learned on this day that marked the death of Mr. Woods and my inclusion in the Civil Rights Movement. The game of tennis taught me well as a child and it continues to do so. Be a sport when losing and especially when winning. Reinforce self-reliance learned as a kid in the face of homesickness, close scores, teasing, bad calls, and gossip. Never give up, play fair, respect opponents, be grateful for every opportunity, and embrace plain good luck.

Gratitude washed over me as I recalled all the carpools, road trips, parental chaperoning and hosting of out-of-town players at 1203. Oceanfront family vacations were willingly sacrificed for courtside seats at yet another tournament in another town. My father's heartening reminder whenever I faced tall odds on the court that "On a given day, anything is possible" remains my go-to mantra. Yes, thank you, one and all, from this grateful recipient of infinite, unconditional generosity. Stay with me evermore, this saturating gratitude.

I remembered that pivotal day and experienced its emotions as vividly as if I were dressing for the big match this morning. Patting Billy awake, I felt a rush of gratitude for this champ of a pup, too.

On the late afternoon drive back to Charlottesville, I replayed a wondrous tennis postscript. Not long ago, I headed home to Richmond to accept an award and give a talk at the Westwood Club, scene of many youthful tennis tournaments. While relaxing in the foyer, I turned to look up at the large painting poised directly above my chair. Holy smoke. In a lifelike portrait of "Richmond's Mr. Tennis," the fingers of his right hand spread precisely over the length of the grip while his left hand gently cradled the racquet at its throat. His hair slicked back as I saw it only for my big matches, Mr. Woods exuded love for his game. Collecting myself for my speech, I noticed the sign above the door across from his portrait. I entered the "Wimbledon Room" for the luncheon. Mr. Woods, Wimbledon, and me. Yep, Dad, "On a given day, anything is possible."

What a full, rich circle all of us wove. Thanks, old bedroom closet, for the memories and refresher course. May gratitude rule my life and steer me true.

A "Flexible Flyer," an Old Turtle, and Other Garage Collectibles

Opening Day arrived for The Garage Week Finale at 1203. Zip-A-Dee-Doo-Dah!

Helpers would come and go throughout the five-day adventure, and I tried to envision a vacant cement floor and bare walls come Friday. Garage exploration long provided entertainment for family and friends with its ever-changing, shadowy holdings—shelves, worktables, hooks, buckets, jars, rafters—unlimited stowing potential in addition to ground space. "Just put it in the garage" answered countless queries for fifty-six years. Mac organized and rearranged steadfastly, lending a semblance of order, but after he died chaos ruled this roost for over two decades. In his absence, I hosted many a garage party on return trips home, a weekend of partially clearing out the one-car garage no vehicle ever entered. The garage refilled seemingly on its own, growing stealthily from spacious to jammed, and I'd send out party invitations once again.

This simple building, so remarkable for us apartment dwellers, harbored the remnants of our time at 1203. I dreaded garage emptying. Under its roof I'd uncover souvenirs of everyone's younger days. What would we have done without our deluxe storage shed? And what would I do with it today?

The driveway originally consisted of gravel that spewed under the tires of rookie visitors, its beaten path regularly requiring additional rocks poured into thinning spots. Frequent guests praised the paving of the drive, and at the finish line Mac carved "McC, 1960" into the garage's new cement base. Our various used vehicles pulled up the driveway to its end at the closed garage doors, the back gate to the right and a row of crape myrtles soon planted on the left. The pioneering car was a lumbering white two-door Ford station wagon nicknamed Moby Dick, its back seat folding down into a makeshift dormitory for Patrick and me, its whitewall tires a touch of class. Wedged next to Moby in front of the garage, a green Packard sedan smelled of another century and chugged along at buggy speed. A soft green, reliable Ford Fairlane parked here a long time, paling in comparison to everyone's favorite, Satin Doll, a gold VW convertible with wire rim wheels that June sported around town until the floorboard gave way. On special occasions in high school, it was mine— top down glory days, radio turned up, stick shift and clutch dancing in sync with The Beach Boys' "Little Deuce Coupe." I learned from experience about the lever on the floor, flipping it to activate the emergency fuel supply for a stalled car without a gas gauge.

I walked with Billy from the patio around the garage. A framed window centers the side facing our back yard, the window's gray trim setting off the soft yellow of the garage, and as always plentiful pink and white petunias bloom in a window box with day lilies clustered below. The window opens from the outside with the twist of a knob—I pictured an old radio just inside, reachable by kids for station and volume control. Bracketing the window, a ceramic sun and a metal crescent moon salute nearby patio revelers day and night. Rounding the corner, I checked the fig tree shading the back of the garage, our perennial summer delicacies almost ripe.

Leaving the backyard, Billy and I circled around my parked car to the far side of the garage. Without window or decoration and facing an open expanse in the 1205 yard, this side provided us with a multi-sport playground. It doubled as a backboard while I served buckets of tennis balls and booted a kickball with school chums. We invented a scary game of dodgeball with the target's back to this wall. My uncle crouched here with his catcher's mitt, Roger pounding the empty glove as another overthrown ball banged against our garage backstop.

I moved my car to the bottom of the driveway, thinking on my way up that it lacked the character of Moby and Doll. I stood in the open area at the front of the garage and recalled every detail of my cherished basketball court. Long before purple wisteria grew above the two garage doors, even before pavement replaced gravel, the installation of a basketball hoop thrilled my every day. A thick white backboard supported the bright orange rim and crisp white net. The setup offered me sweet incentive to get good, fast. Dribbling the big ball with small hands, I hit uneven turf on every bounce. Despite my "squared up" professional stance, shots fell short as they arced uphill toward a hoop higher than regulation in any league. When my feel for the lay of this land improved, I finally hit the bottom of the net, then managed to reach the side of the backboard. Months passed and my flat shots now clanged off the rim and caromed past me unpredictably, rolling down the driveway with little blocking help from mailbox, bushes, or nearby cars. I could control the ball only by making a basket, the ball slowly trickling through the net into my happy grasp. When I made the basketball team in eighth grade, this official game—low basket, level wood floor, teammates, referees—seemed tame in comparison to garage ball. Though I played hoops in high school, college, and coached this game, no contest was more fun than h-o-r-s-e played on my hilly home court. Double or nothing.

Pacing around the outskirts of the old court, putting off the inevitable, I longed to switch places with ten-year-old me. Quickly so as not to lose resolve, I removed the unlocked latch and the doors swung wide. Yikes. The garage's carrying capacity swelled to an eyepopping peak. Propping the doors open with bricks, I stepped tentatively into the 1203 lawn and garden center—several sizes of clippers and kinds of rakes, a pitchfork, birdfeeders and suet holders, a saw and an axe, both gasoline and push mowers, and an empty fuel can with long spout. Two wheelbarrows contained bags of mulch and watering cans. Old bicycles leaned together against a wall, a boy's and a girl's, the tires flat but not hopeless. Both kickstands working, baskets secured on the front, the bells on the handlebars still ringing. Placing a foot here and twisting around there, I made my slow way around short and tall ladders, big jars of unidentifiable liquids, and boxes of *Gourmet* magazines. My reflection in large antique mirrors startled me every time. I stared back, inventing their histories and momentarily reinventing my own.

Pocketing a key for roller skates I wouldn't find, I stopped abruptly at the sight of seven animal-shaped ceramic planters in a corner, almost hidden by several bags of potting soil surrounding them for protection. I turned an elephant and a frog upside down, yearning to see on the bottom the carved initials of dear friends of yesteryear. Handling each one with care as I set it aside, I anticipated revisiting these planters, one in particular.

I wiggled out of the garage carrying an old sewing table, measurements carved on its edges, perfect for our lunch spread. June's caregiver Janet dropped off her four teenage grandchildren, a hardworking and jolly quartet. Two septuagenarian family friends pulled up in a ramshackle van, borrowed for today's trips to the dump. My former college students each brought a pal new to me and 1203. Incredulity marked the faces of first-time garage partyers while regulars chuckled at the scene of another jamboree. Our group of ten helpers closed ranks. The laidback crew introduced themselves, shaking hands and slapping backs while snatching cold drinks from coolers. Instant good cheer perked up the garage environs and my spirit. The plan was simple. Begin. Endure. Discover. Party.

My former basketball court transformed as helpers toted out an infinite variety of items. Occasionally standing back, I observed the procession in and out of the garage. I was enchanted by everyone's unexpected sensitivity. Cries of "Found a Treasure!" or "Check this out!" rang out often. A lovely hum swelled the heart I wore on my sleeve. Somehow, each person intuited the nonmonetary value for me of these little and big, strange and funny, all together poignant things. They sensed that items discarded many years ago had once been pieces of our lives. No one made fun of a deflated red and white ABA basketball. No one called a rusty birdcage junk or laughed at the long line of coffee cans containing rusted screws, nails, and bolts. Cheers greeted the sight of our first and still rolling "Radio Flyer" red wagon with black wheels and handle. The nimble teenagers climbed over and slipped around whatever blocked their paths, hauling three trunks stacked toward the back into the light. The first, smallest one belonged to Italian translator EJ and bore the insignia of the State Department in Rome—the same trunk that accompanied me when I set out for college. The other two were the property of Lt. Edward J. McCarty, shipped ahead of his homecoming from military service. I pried open my dad's as silent friends looked on. One safeguarded a crisply-folded US flag, the other a woolen blanket in mint condition with "US NAVY" stenciled at each end.

I flat-out hooted as we came upon not a few boxes of unused toilet seats with lids, small groupings secured in various hiding places. "Here's another one!" Giddy and hungry, we concocted fables of the emergencies Mac foresaw, the contests he maybe won, or the bargains he'd stumbled upon and kept to himself. This improbable topic of our group confab sparked more storytelling.

Garage collectibles everywhere, we circled for lunch on the shaded driveway, some sitting on the trunks and others on park benches. Stories and sandwiches, iced tea and camaraderie. Tales of inventory taken at other garages matched this one, almost. Several people new to 1203 described the process of emptying their own family homes while the youngest among us pondered the prospect for the first time. We applauded a kazoo-like demonstration of "playing the comb," a septuagenarian remembering his dad teaching him this wax paper skill. Having spotted my first radio—plastic, mauve, and tinny sounding—I bragged about its ability to pick up late night tunes on Buffalo's WKBW. Bemused, respectful millennials grinned, their heads cocked at tales from olden times. We pretend-ordered a flavor while examining the hand crank of Plum's ice cream maker. My friends wistfully named their beloved toys while rocking Gallop, Patrick's hobby horse. Talk of loved and missed parents and grandparents—their quirks, hobbies, and special talents—lightened loads and wound us together. Story sharing fostered compassion as we joked and bumped shoulders. We worked contentedly in silence, too.

Three more hours of labor and everyone stopped simultaneously, as if on command—enough for this opening day in July. We grabbed wood folding chairs from the garage and kicked back with hard-earned beverages. All done and very pleased with ourselves, the trunks now served as foot stools. After loading the dump-bound van one last time, exchanging sweaty hugs and promises to meet again, we parted company. Day one down, four to go. Now, at last, I could spend alone time with an old turtle.

I carried the ceramic planters, chipped and stained in places but flush with rich history, around from the side of the garage. The planters had brightened all our rooms, showcasing shamrock variations, ponytail plants, an amaryllis or orchid. June proudly brought newbies home. These glazed elephant, frog, turtle, and starfish cache pots took me back to another home on a hill, this one on the other side of Fountain Lake from the Byrd Park tennis courts. I opened the door to The Virginia Home.

The mission of The Home remains lifelong care for adults with permanent physical disabilities. Hooked on the place as a volunteer, June worked full-time for several years in the Occupational Therapy Room. Her relaxed, genuine relationships with the residents moved me. Wheelchairs jostled for first dibs in the noisy room, my mother poured molds for firing in a big kiln, and volunteers helped residents paint ceramic beauties. Tiger, June's toy poodle, presided. After teaching or playing tennis during college summers, I fetched her from work—glad for the extra time to spend with my friends until June's shift ended.

I received an incomparable education at The Home, where residents played the hand dealt with style, grace, and humor. Each individual won my heart as I watched one after another seize every joy possible. I drifted around the enormous building, partying in the big room for birthdays and bingo, visiting ailing residents in their private rooms, pushing a wheelchair outside for a stroll. When I pulled around The Home's circular drive, the first sight of my pals waiting for me on the veranda knotted my throat. How kind they were, asking about the tennis tournament, my weekend plans, the date of my return to college. They regaled me with tall tales of the Elvis concert, an outing organized by my intrepid mother. Residents in wheelchairs cruised up the automatic lift of their new bus, "Genie," and off they went with staff members to Richmond's Mosque to hear "Jailhouse Rock" and "Don't Be Cruel." I got the scoop on June's most recent caper, a surprise shindig to celebrate the installation of an automatic door for the OT room. "Your mother can always find a reason to party!" Jimmy, a boy my age, laughed.

Yes, it was these residents' initials I had sought on the planters. I picked up the ceramic turtle for closer inspection. How extraordinary, this tale of now two turtles. Not long ago, I met this one's sibling, filled with lush philodendron, in Pine Knolls, North Carolina. Walking into the library to give a talk, my breath caught when I saw the turtle on a table. My host Barbara worked her first job at my mother's side, firing up the kiln and throwing parties. New to Pine Knolls forty-five years later, she spotted the turtle at her first book club meeting hosted at its owner's house. "I know that turtle!" she screamed. She kindly invited the turtle and its proud owner to my reading. How beautiful to listen as Barbara introduced me, telling the audience stories about her job long ago and this fabulous woman named June, and then hearing "and this is June's daughter" as my cue to speak.

I arranged the planters on the trunks, good omens to greet tomorrow's work gang. As I was closing the garage doors, a truck revved up the driveway, Billy's tail wagging helicopter-style the sign of a frequent visitor. Rewarding him with pats and a treat, the handyman who specialized in garage inspection and repair expressed sorrow at June's death and offered his help. "I'm wild about old things and couldn't get enough of your mother's stories about the history of this and the uses for that." He retold June's stories, some brand new to me. And then he uttered these words. "We finally ran out of room in the loft."

The loft?

Wordlessly, he pointed and we looked up. The four-sided garage boasted a fifth dimension. June's agent grabbed a ladder, an original fixture in the garage, and shakily up he climbed. "I love this one most of all!" he said, lowering our "Flexible Flyer" sled. Oh, this magnificent sturdy plaything of winters past, it ferried Patrick and me, layered atop Mac, down the paved driveway. A year later we steered the Flyer down twisty, steep back roads near the University of Richmond.

Today's interactions bathed me in kindness. Kindness changes lives—it changed mine today. Dish it out. Let it rip.

Quite a big day—an old turtle buddy and the world's best sled.

"Found two treasures."

Picnic Baskets and Camping Gear

Hooray! Two cars parked at the top of the driveway, just like the old days, promised a cheery start to a hot late-June day. My cousin Matthew and my mother's and now my friend Floyd, drinking coffee on the patio, greeted Billy and me at the back gate. The two born comedians joked and carried on, setting us up for a playful workday.

As soon as he could walk, little boy Matthew looked for any reason to go to the basement, and today's assignment gave him another excuse. "Come on down!" Matthew yelled up from the basement, and Floyd jumped at the partylike invitation. I stayed on the patio reading days of accumulated mail until the sounds of workers-at-play lured me downstairs. The moment I spotted the shelf filled with picnic baskets, I settled on my "task."

Childhood memories of outdoor feasts flashed by like scenes in a favorite movie. As far back as my recall stretches, its viewfinder zooms in on picnics. In rumpled photographs my great-grandfather, dressed in his Sunday-best three-piece suit, tucked his long legs under an already packed picnic table. Generations later, Maria's photographs made my mouth water—her homemade picnic spread for family caravanning to her niece Madeleine's college graduation. Picnics are us.

My heart swelled at the sight of the worn wicker harbingers of good times. Giving each dear basket a swing, I found colorful tablecloths with matching cloth napkins in some, and a mishmash of my mother's endless supply of cocktail napkins in others. Crinkled wax paper, saved for another day, lay among rubber bands and metal rings from Mason jars. I rubbed small crumbs between my fingers, smelling non-existent leftovers. No two baskets looked alike—ribbons streaming from some handles, a few baskets adorned with hand-painted wood tops—and the solid lid of my grandmother's Peterboro often doubled as a small table.

Floyd and Matthew stayed mostly on task while I shuffled around the chatty duo—a young girl, secretly picnic-bound again. Family picnics started early and lasted long, each part of the ritual obeyed. Everyone talked and nobody listened while preparing and packing goodies, the buzzing commotion the picnic's soundtrack. Wax paper and aluminum foil were cut to spec for wrapping sandwiches, extra sheets packed for leftovers. Picnic prep bounced along in an easy groove—bottled drinks and an ice chest, reusable plates and cups, paper and dish towels, mismatched silverware and glasses, bottle opener and corkscrew, binoculars and cameras, tongs and slatted spoons, toothpicks and tablecloths. Cries of "No Sampling," in the midst of tempting smells, were ignored completely—senior chef Plum broke her halfhearted command, chewing while issuing it. Thermoses filled to the brim with lemonade, water, and iced tea, their tops too wide for unscrewing by sneaky children's hands. The cap of the skinniest, tallest thermos also served as a stainless-steel cup—this thermos usually reserved for hot coffee and occasionally (I found out the easy way) for chilled white wine.

Time for take-off. Hands snagged hats hanging from pegs at the top of the basement stairs—baseball, straw, floppy canvas, visors—if chilly, choices of ski caps and scarves. Best of all, Plum donned a tea cosy as her knitted blue bonnet. Arriving at our destination, the car unpacked in a flurry. Yum. Some combo of these standbys awaited us veteran picnickers: fried chicken, deviled eggs, potato salad, cole slaw, pickles and olives, cashews and pistachios. Thin white bread sandwiches, layered with slivers of Vidalia onion or cucumbers, dressed with mayonnaise and a sprinkling of cayenne pepper (I always snuck one for the road), baguettes for assorted cheeses, and crackers for pimiento. Smithfield ham biscuits, sliced tomatoes with olive oil and fresh basil, celery and carrot sticks, baked beans in an orange ceramic pot with glazed handles on its sides. Peach cobbler or chess pie or lemon tarts or strawberries or all and more.

Sometimes we (they, the grownups) agreed on a destination—the Blue Ridge Parkway or Skyline Drive, a park or wilderness area, river bank or hillside, mountain peak or ocean, a garden or meadow. Unless weather interfered, spontaneous picnics broke up long car trips, riders' eyes peeled for a beckoning pull-over spot. Places along the way sprung up just in time—our unofficial rest areas established quickly and artfully on a rock wall or to the side of a rural road with the back of the station wagon serving as a stand-around table. Family and friends traveled picnic routes from Virginia to Massachusetts to Florida to Maryland to anywhere. Occasionally we swapped food and conversation with other picnickers, learning their hometowns and observing their traditions.

Most of all, I relished the playfulness of these outings—carefree grownups, willfully silly, my childlike contemporaries for a day. Nothing dims one particular vision of my grandmother. At some point on our journey, Plum wordlessly stuffed tissues into her ears, apparently her signal that the car radio prevented her from hearing the backseat conversation. Seen from behind, her ears closely resembled a cocker spaniel's. Mac turned off the radio, all of us laughing long and hard except his smirking, dogeared passenger. I was enthralled by their stories of people and places I'd never know, outdoor adventures long ago now brand new.

Indeed, talk of picnics past and future gladdened and comforted my mother during her last hospital stay.

Morning passed quickly. Footsteps in the kitchen above announced lunch delivery from another funny friend, Marguerite, whom I met at June's bank. Marguerite snatched a sunhat from the old cache, a fashionable complement to the old-time hats we chose that morning—Matthew wearing one of Plum's straw hats with painted flowers, Floyd hiding under Mac's sombrero, me not nearly as stylish as Big Daddy in his straw boater. Our quartet feasted in a shady area on the patio with Billy underfoot, eager for his fair share of spilled treats.

The appeal of open air never lost its draw for my family. Friends, like Floyd and Marguerite, caught the outdoor fever, too. Whenever possible, we figured out a way for gathering outdoors or at the very least for bringing fresh air inside 1203. Just a smidgen of a crack in bedroom windows, even and especially in winter, delivered us cold breaths of crisp air. At the first hint of springtime, we pried loose and raised high partially-stuck windows. Reluctantly, we sealed 1203 shut on summer's hottest days, two window units and ceiling fans cooling the house. Windows and doors flung wide open in autumn.

Our banker's lunch hour at an end, we returned to our basement jobs. My helpers' morning work had opened up floor space, and we could now pull out taller items from the back wall. I didn't recognize a large rattan "basket" that required the three of us to free from surrounding boxes and furniture and hoist into the open area. We unhooked the braided latches and peered inside, unveiling everything needed for a campout "kitchen." Both the inside of the lid and the deep lower section revealed cleverly layered and stacked tin cooking equipment for outdoor use—plates, cups, coffee pot, a range of pans and pots, eating utensils, ladles and knives, and long-handled spoons for stirring the biggest pots. Imagine carrying this formidable collection to the campsite and knowing what to do with it. Gadzooks.

Plum carried it and Plum knew it all.

What a bonus for us to revisit the legend of the famous camping trip embarked upon by camp master Plum, her grandson Patrick, and his neighborhood friend Bobby. Our treasure trophy of the day was taped along one side of the big basket. I carefully unpeeled an article from the *Richmond Times-Dispatch* dated September 6, 1963 entitled "Mountain-Climbing Grandmother Camps Out with Youngsters." The lengthy piece saluted the trio's five-day adventure in the Shenandoah National Park in an area named Big Meadows. Photographs accompanying the article, taken by Bobby, captured the spirit of the expedition—a perfectly pitched canvas tent, kerosene lamp, clothes tossed over tree branches to dry, Plum pouring an open can into a pot over their campfire, Patrick handing her supplies while sitting in the trunk of the car, a couple of water buckets, a small refrigerator.

Matthew and Floyd pulled out chairs and we sat around our make-believe campsite. I read aloud the hilarious article, rereading the knockout lines on the spot.

"Look what's happened to the image of American grandmothers. No more cameos and lace collars, shawls have been tossed aside and rocking chairs are reserved for the younger generation. 'It was the hardest thing I've ever done and I LIKE roughing it,' said Hilda Smith, nodding her neatly bouffanted steel-gray head emphatically. 'Animals and insects don't bother me. If it's an insect, just brush it off. If it's an animal, shoo it off.' Neither brushing or shooing worked with whatever it was that ate its way through Patrick's father's raincoat in an attempt to rob their portable refrigerator. 'I'm tough,' the short, little widow repeated, 'but Old Rag (3,291-foot-high mountain) was the greatest challenge of my life. Once on rocks near the top, I heard someone's foot slip.' She would have slipped herself had not a muscular stranger given her a boost from below, she added." I stopped reading and joined in the hysterics.

I camped out once. Since that rainy, foggy, tent-leaking, downward-slope sleeping, latrine-seeking-in-the-dark adventure, I consider stays in a rural hotel my camping trips. But I'd go camping for a month with fearless Plum just to hear the "short, little widow" comment on her "neatly bouffanted" self.

Matthew gently fingered the faded newspaper clipping like a valuable historical document, a story of his grandmother's exploits dated a few months before he was born. As we passed the article around and examined it closely, two bolded headings drew our attention: "Forest Rangers Were Searching" and "Hair Dryer Was Victim." When the intrepid campers hadn't pulled up the 1203 driveway at the expected, agreed upon, oft-repeated time, my parents called the local police who alerted the park rangers. Their ambitious climb up "Old Rag" and slow trek down had delayed their departure, a Ranger's phone call assured, but they were now safely headed home. From my bedroom I heard the triumphant campers' boisterous midnight return.

The roles of the forest rangers now clear, I read twice the section on the victimized hair dryer. My mother explained to the reporter the extent of her worry for her twelve-year-old child and his companions. Then, relieved and loosening up, June elaborated, "You could say he spent the week in my hair dryer." The interviewer, surely requesting an explanation, continued. "Mrs. McCarty gave up nearly three years' worth of trading stamps for Patrick to buy his air mattress, canteen, and sleeping bag." Those were the days of saving S&H green and Tru-Value yellow stamps, slowly earned with purchases at grocery stores, and June's goal was a new hair dryer.

The image of Patrick sleeping in a hair dryer reminded me that our mother June McCarty possessed a funny bone for the ages.

We took a break. I walked around the neighborhood with Billy and that funny girl June.

My mother loved the world and it loved her right back. When she died at eighty-nine, high school pal Molly spoke for all my friends: "She was the first one of our moms who made me laugh. You always felt so sophisticated when she treated you as if you were grown up enough to understand one of her asides." That hair dryer sense of humor never abandoned her. Humor was her ally while carpooling, dancing, answering telemarketers' calls, rearranging furniture, and during every blow to her health. June's readiness to laugh at herself infused her with becoming humility—her laugh in the mirror rewarded her with wise, big-picture perspective. She rode tall through ups or downs, steadied during joy and hardship, and indulged in life's simplest, purest pleasures. Her intelligent wit anchored her in an obviously contented life.

Floyd, Matthew, and I picked up where we left off, lazing around the big camping hamper. We shared first one then another comical June story, laughing hard in the telling. One recent example of her self-effacing humor leapt immediately to mind. A phone call from a credit card representative, alerting June that her card had been used for fraudulent purchases in Florida, confused and alarmed her. Reassured by the caller, then by visiting Maria, then by me on the phone that all was well and the "criminal's charges" wouldn't appear on her bill, June let out a relieved sigh during our call. "You know what I will never understand? The thief charged a thousand dollars at an apple store. What on earth could anyone possibly do with that many apples?" After an unusually long silence on my end, I explained to my mom the particulars of a certain kind of Apple Store. Another long silence, this time on her end—and then her low chuckle quickly gave way to cries of laughter that tickled the phone in my hand. Finally, she found her words: "Would any-body but crazy me not know this? Not even my mother could can that many apples."

We basked in her sense of humor the rest of our workday. Yes, an arch of her eyebrow and a room erupted in laughter. A bare-ly-audible phrase uttered to her companion at the dinner table and it was her guffawing seatmate who took the fall. June never told a joke, that wasn't her style. A natural, she made no effort to be amus-ing. Her humor soared with understatement, dry as brine, clever as a favorite song's lyrics, memorable as the best gift you ever received. When Matthew headed back to northern Virginia and Floyd to his home in the country, we bade grinning farewells. And I reveled in a rare worry-free ride back to Charlottesville that evening.

How energizing to enjoy a young-at-heart workday. My mother refreshed others' lives just as she beautified her own. Even as we emptied her beloved home, she made us merry today. Un-intentionally and all her life, she taught me unforgettable lessons through her beguiling penchant for fun. I watched it work for her, day in and day out, sustaining her zest for life as it lifted heavy hearts. Her knack for using humor as remedy never devolved into sarcasm or cruelty—rooted in good will, its use always appropriate and light-hearted.

Laughing out loud at her extravagant apple purchase, I re-solved not to lose my sense of humor, ever, especially this summer. Nonstop willingness to laugh at myself will set me straight—and when I lose my way, I can recalibrate my path with humor's help. I'll go nowhere near my wit's end.

Billy and I got back to our Charlottesville home right at sun-set. My usual weary step after a home-emptying day now clicked with a spanking new pop.

The Grill and a Ping Pong Table

1203 boasted a "great room" well before its time. Our most popular space emerged in fits and starts from the back of the house, eventually spreading the home's width and encompassing half of the backyard. The branches of two oaks created its umbrella roof, the floor laid in varying shapes of blue slate set in concrete, its walls of flowers and bushes grown higher each year. The patio, lit by sun and moon, hosted four appreciative generations. Ruled by dogs, watched over by birds, overrun by acorn-seeking squirrels, it was the place to be.

Movers unloading the truck fifty-six years ago trod a precarious path through the gate to the back door. Pulling heavy loads on dollies, carrying our big furniture with their vision blocked, they stepped cautiously over or around gnarly tree roots and isolated clumps of grass. Our first backyard chairs rocked unpredictably and the kitchen served as a precursor to modern "mud rooms." The patio's modest beginnings appeared as soon as time and money allowed. A slate trail extended straight out from the back stoop and wrapped around a newly-planted flower bed that circled a big oak. What a haven, this party area that in a few years stretched all the way from the back gate to the opposite fence. Before it reached its glorious full width, on the far side we planted two white dogwood trees that filtered late afternoon sun. Mac and Patrick built a serpentine cobblestone border—ten inches at its highest and four inches at its lowest points—separating the patio from a somewhat grassy backyard. Small garden patches, interrupted by a semicircle of tiny boxwood bushes, formed the winding patio perimeter behind their nifty stone barrier.

The patio doubled as an oasis reserved exclusively for relaxation. If possible, we were there—fiddling with homework, waiting for a ride, playing with a dog—amusing ourselves without a care. Grownups sipped morning coffee and Friday night cocktails. In this summer of home emptying, the patio drew its usual crowd with most days beginning and ending here. We enjoyed lunch and laughter under the dogwoods' canopy, shared tales and emotions, Billy at home in his world.

After a solid week of sorting and boxing, I welcomed the opportunity for a change of scene—especially since this particular work would focus on our outdoor home, the patio and backyard. Often in the early days of surveying and planning, I noted needed repairs and waited for a stretch of weather ideally suited to fixit projects that would dress up 1203 for its new residents. As soon as my early-rising friend Amy arrived from Charlottesville, we drove our familiar mile to the neighborhood hardware store. My summer school course in home maintenance asked a lot of me this morning, especially the challenging tutorial on repairing cracks in the patio. We loaded Amy's van with concrete mending materials plus bags of fill dirt to remedy holes in the backyard—smaller divots carved by mallets and putters, more treacherous ones dug by sly dogs determined to access the garage from below. We purchased wire brushes, primer, and spray paint to spruce up outdoor furniture for the patio's last summer on my watch. Equipped for our tasks, we headed home.

After a full day's work and intermittent play, we stopped and admired our progress, two amateurs relieved that faithful Floyd, a truly handy man, had surprised us with a few hours of his expert help. Sure enough, paint dried and cement hardened. Amy and Billy checked out the filled holes, strolled around the yard, and settled in on the patio. I took the garbage out to the old cans tucked behind the garage in a makeshift enclosure shared with our neighbors at 1205 and nocturnal racoons. One bag, more treasure than trash to me, contained remnants uncovered on our eagle-eyed walkabout after lunch—well-chewed rawhide bones, parts of tennis balls chopped by the mower, and fragments of ping pong balls buried in mulch. Tears welled at the sight of my dad's last charcoal grill, rusty and abandoned at the back fence. After inspecting the grill and admitting its unlikely resurrection, I leaned against the garage and studied the grassy backyard area.

I heard happy us. My four younger cousins indulged in summer camp at 1203, the house on the hill transformed into a six-week hostel for six kids and two resident adults. This small backyard playground hosted our Olympic games. Pounding a pocket into softening mitts, we caught short pop flies and slapped a glove on crazy-bounding grounders. Mini-croquet tournaments featured disappearing wickets and spur-of-the-moment partner swaps. We pitched first rubber then metal horseshoes. Lounging on the patio, adults cheered passionate Wiffle ball contests. Frisbees flew—tag, you're it. After one glimpse at our reckless attempt at Red Rover, June canceled its season.

Slipping between two now-hefty boxwoods back onto the patio, I rejoined my dawn-to-dusk companions. My tired friend Amy stretched full length on a bench and Billy propped his chin on a tennis ball. We embraced the 1203 patio technique of doing nothing, lolling contentedly in an area that looked much as it did fifty years ago. I left them in the present and switched back to my teenaged self.

It's late Saturday afternoon and my father bends low behind a mower, acorns crunching underfoot, a dog nipping at his heels—the backyard being readied for tomorrow's cookout. Come Sunday, Patrick lies in our treasured Pawleys Island hammock, tethered between the two big oak trees—one towering in the center of the patio, the other reaching skyward just beyond the border wall in a raised bed of jonquils. Around the side of the far oak, a basket swing faces away from the patio, swaying with an occasional push from Daniel's pale blue high tops. June totes cushions for Salterini wrought iron chairs and benches, tying the pads at the back, plumping pillows here and situating small tables there. Mac grabs the partially-coiled hose and rewinds it completely, heading out for the quick trip to pick up Big Daddy at the bus stop. Cousins rub shoulders on the glider. Plum arrives with trays of ramekins brimming with flan for dessert, admiring the glass-topped tables she once used in Florida. EJ chats with Roger on a white bench, but only after she has emptied watering cans and clipped fresh herbs for today's feast. Neighbors to the left and right wave hello and wander over for however long. Friends just happen to drive by this house on a dead-end street and pop in, claiming a recliner or a director's chair.

Mac, master of the backyard grill and the art of taking it easy, set the tone. He held court in a lawn chair by the grill, his permanent station positioned near the two dogwoods. He savored his Sunday routine—flipping through the morning paper, surveying the patio, making sure the hammock pillow lay on the safer end in case of an inadvertent tumble. He shuffled around in his trademark loafers with no socks, stopping what he wasn't doing to low-five kids and fill shallow pewter bowls with Virginia peanuts. After a while, my pop ambled to the gate with a hearty greeting for all, granting each beverage request and passing a cheeseboard. Mid-afternoon stomach rumbles coincided with the start of Mac's grilling ritual. Long before store-bought "chimney starters," my father fashioned one from a Maxwell House coffee can. After removing the bottom, he punched holes along the sides at the base. Placing his "starter" in the well of the grill, he covered the base with a small wad of newspaper, loaded the can with charcoal, and lit a tip of paper. A gentle, timed puff or two from the chef and presto, a red glow. After dumping the hot coals, he used tongs to arrange them just so, adding more as needed for roasting a big-time Sunday supper. The grill simmered. Birds sang. Plum issued a Scrabble game challenge. Mac listened in on various conversations as he repositioned a coal or two. I waited for my secret opening—the customary lull before grilling. Now! I picked up a paddle and ball.

Not far from the grill lay my queendom—our homemade ping pong table, supported by two sturdy lumber "horses," steadied on the most level patio area near the far fence. I'd prepared the playing field first thing that morning. At both ends, paddles rested at an angle on balls. The taut net, anchored by screws underneath the table on either side, measured to professional regulations. This one-of-a-kind table assured me home field advantage. Its white center line zigzagged, its warped tilt invisible to all but the most discerning, its painted-over dents and chips known only to me. Not once did I tire of this game played to twenty-one points, must win by two. In my dreams I toyed with all comers, cagily hitting a short angle or whipping topspin to move my opponent over uneven footing. I used any breeze, pile of acorns, all flower pots, and even the hot grill to my advantage. Unfazed birds and squirrels tangled in their own competition on a feeder hanging overhead in a dogwood. What a nice break from the tennis court, these hours of table tennis played barefoot, the ball never rolling far away, merry patio partyers the backdrop. I'm still game.

I couldn't have known then that on these lazy Sundays I was memorizing lessons far more important than measuring geometry angles or avoiding dangling prepositions. Nothing beats a day without agenda, a special time set aside for companionship and play, a standing reservation for freewheeling leisure. I counted the days till our Sunday slowdown. Now, calling time-out always takes me home. An intentional getaway, come what may, fine tunes the rhythm of my life. No race—no finish line. Alive.

Paddles down. Rising smoke signaled time for specific activities. Everyone pitched in. The kitchen screen door snapped open and closed—fleet feet or long arms a requirement. Green, pink, and white tablecloths draped over round, square, and rectangular tables, followed by plates, glasses, and utensils that set the scene. Making several trips to the kitchen, Mac brought out Pyrex bowls of chicken—basted in lemon, rosemary, olive oil, and June's secret sauce—and a big tray stacked with ears of buttered corn wrapped in foil. The last platter out held an array of colorful skewers—a couple with short cuts of Kielbasa, plenty with peppers, onions, zucchini, and mushrooms, and two with eggplant chunks for grownups. June's kitchen prep matched grill readiness like clockwork. Platters of Hanover tomatoes topped with vinaigrette and basil, a big bowl of June's potato salad garnished with parsley, pitchers of tea and lemonade, a bottle of red wine and another of white completed the menu. Mealtime ignored real time. We ate and talked, returned for seconds, talked and ate. No child ever asked "May I be excused, please?" After savoring Plum's flan, diners cleared tables, washed and dried dishes, lit candles, drank coffee, flopped into hammock and chairs. Children of all ages inched rows of marshmallows up the ends of improvised coat hanger spears, roasting a second dessert over embers. Time kept patio pace.

While spontaneity sparked most patio gatherings, planning and setup for special occasions stretched out the fun for weeks. Under the oaks we celebrated Patrick's high school graduation and his engagement party, toasted Plum's ninety-fifth birthday and Daniel's marriage, saluted homecomings and bon voyages. Slim, wooden folding chairs, piled high inside the front of the garage, transported easily under arms or on children's heads for bigger get-togethers.

How appropriate that our cherished patio hosted the last parties honoring June and Mac. Since our first year in college Eleanor called 1203 home. When she returned from Florida one last time for June's memorial garden party, May 4, 2013, she swung a mini white suitcase as she high-stepped up the driveway, the same pretend valise carried long ago on her first visit. As Eleanor was leaving, she confided to me that she "planted" a special marble beneath a certain tree—the tree that she had ordered as a surprise for Mac's farewell gathering on April 10, 1991. Rolling open the doors of his truck parked outside the back gate, a deliveryman read Eleanor's card for all on the patio to hear: "Is this Mac's favorite place?" Yes. What a sight for sad eyes and highlight of the party—a strapping white dogwood, its myriad blooms about to pop open, new life for 1203. June chose the spot—at the very top of the front yard, visible from the living room window and the sunporch—and late that afternoon Daniel planted his uncle Mac's tree.

I scoped out Mac's realm today, bare feet cooled by irregular flagstones, and felt the pure contentment that we patio lovers knew by heart. The world entertained us. I marvel, now, that I never heard June or Mac utter the irksome phrase "I'm too busy." My parents and grandparents worked hard. Surely financial worries loomed at times. They may have been exhausted, many responsibilities to meet, but never too busy. We took time and spent it.

Plum's great-grandchildren found Mac's favorite place enticing, too. Maria's children Will and Nelson hung out here—exploring, lying in mounds of leaves, their curious fingers detecting the buried yellow plaque warning "chipmunk crossing." With her middle name McCarty, perhaps it was inevitable that Jonathan's daughter Madeleine would inherit her dad's love of 1203. She often overnighted with June and Billy for days at a time, telling me that "I just want to spend every minute I can there. My favorite thing of all is Billy leading me on long walks, sprinting up the driveway home, and seeing June waiting for us on the patio. She has treats for Billy and me, every single time." Thirteen-year-old Madeleine and her octogenarian great-aunt, Billy and his bone. A fourth generation got it right, too.

While Amy and Billy played the parts of after-cookout patio snoozers, I gave in to the powerful sensory impressions that washed over me. I sat with my grinning father, a slow cook gleefully divorced from his banker role, and the aftertaste of charred marshmallows lingered on my burnt tongue. I tasted his leftover barbecued chicken, packed for my Monday lunch to classmates' envy. Fresh cut grass mingling with faint gas mower fumes smelled of summer. The carillon from the nearby church provided year-round patio music, the number of chimes tolling at the top of the hour the only timekeeper we heeded—and the church bells announcing eight o'clock on this evening echoed the notes of my youth. As a child I delighted in the woofing of first one and then another neighborhood dog, barking on cue in their call and response chorus. I pretended to understand their language, wanting to be part of their world—and I listened tonight as another band struck up and Billy harmonized in his high-pitched voice. Crickets chirped and a frog croaked, interrupted by the disquieting siren from the fire station not far away—the same sounds of a half century ago. I was overwhelmed and overjoyed.

It grew dark on the patio. Ah, yes, outdoor nighttime gatherings give me back my childhood. When I glean the inviting hum of easygoing, starlit conversations, I hear once more those loved voices of yesteryear, naturally lowered as the sun set on the patio—Sunday's warm, soothing timbre at closing time. Lightning bugs blink, globes protect candles from the wind, clusters of votives burn low. The moon, from sliver to round, lights the night. The Little Dipper befriends me as ever. And the North Star fascinates and comforts as it did when I twirled a ping pong paddle, reassuring in its consistency, a sign that I can always find my way home. On the 1203 patio I first marveled that the earth was spinning, and I sought any inkling of movement with bare feet planted on blue slate. Nighttime is the right time to plant bare feet again.

Come, let's dawdle. Swing with me. Stand still, time. Tickle my fancy, North Star.

Christmas Tree Stands and One Tall Rabbit

Billy lay at my feet, a sluggish pup after hours of barking at last night's Fourth of July fireworks. We made a slow pair this morning, a melancholy mood overtaking me after experiencing my first holiday alone in an emptying home.

We so looked forward to holiday celebrations, each one with its distinctive call to revelry. Yesterday I missed the patio cookouts that marked Independence Day—a flag flying from the front stoop, Ruth Jones next door bringing over her orange blossom cupcakes, and all of Billy's predecessors wild at the first pop of fireworks. Reminiscences of joyful celebrations coursed through me, and soon and surprisingly, I perked up at an infusion of holiday spirit.

Yes! Ringing in a New Year, my funny Valentines, a green

St. Patrick's Day, blooming Easter, happier Independence Days, simply fabulous Thanksgiving, and the grand finale of Christmas. Ignoring Halloween also cheered me up, the one holiday that I avoided best I could. Put off by costumes, I squirmed in embarrassment when insufficiently disguised as cat or clown—a beggar going door-to-door demanding candy. Even cackling June on her broom, sporting her tall witch's hat while answering knocks at the front door, failed to woo me. I was done with trick and treat at age eight. Boo! Let's begin in January.

We lazed into a late breakfast accompanied by the drums and tubas of marching bands on the televised Tournament of Roses Parade. Simmering black-eyed peas and stewed tomatoes ushered in good fortune for the new year—I ate a scant spoonful to bring me luck, preferring oyster stew with little round saltine crackers floating on top. Grownups talked about resolutions and I played along with no intention of making much less keeping any promises. Friends of all ages dropped by throughout the day, guests occasionally performing "Auld Lang Syne" on the piano. Visitors often contributed a plate or pot of their standard New Year's fare—southern staple hoppin john and cornbread, Danish pastries, Dutch oliebollen.

Hearts scattered around the house signaled Valentine's Day, June reminding everyone to keep eyes peeled for heart-shaped rocks—her stone collection still displayed on windowsills and bedside tables. I packed Valentines, made from red construction paper, and a small box of Necco candies in my bookbag. We traded the tiny heart-shaped candies at lunch, handing over chalky, rarely-eaten invitations such as "Kiss me" and "Be Mine." That morning I'd set aside all of the hearts with the misleading message to press in classmates' palms. Innocent of course, I never tired of their expressions as they stared at the words "I'm Sorry."

Chocolate pie with graham cracker crust topped off St. Patrick's Day, the scrumptious finish of our corned beef and cabbage dinner, also the occasion of my fiery introduction to horseradish sauce. Patrick especially enjoyed this day of fun, everyone wearing green in his honor. Mac's best friend, fellow Irishman Russell, joined him in the living room for their off-key rendition of "Too-ra-loo-ra-loo-ra, that's an Irish lullaby." When sung by this duo, "Danny Boy" sounded a chipper tune. I cherished these annual duets, two pals toasting a long friendship that began when their daughters, Sarah and I, bonded on the first day of kindergarten.

What good times my dad and Russ enjoyed together, both spontaneous and planned, with and without their families. From my bedroom I could hear their voices downstairs or on the patio—the comforting drift of their conversations, sometimes low and serious, more often punctuated by bursts of laughter. After Mac's diagnosis, the next afternoon he knocked on Russell's door to deliver in person the hardest news. On the Sunday morning Mac died, his pal Russ and wife Eunice were first through the back gate. More years passed, the threesome continuing their friendship, motoring to Charlottesville for lunch or eating popcorn at matinees. Then, June and I twice returned the sad favor, attending a funeral first for Russ and then Eunice, my kindergarten sleepover chum Sarah weeping like a little girl on June's shoulder. Nothing beats relationships that hold tight through the years—devoted friendships, intentionally given time to grow and deepen.

Ready for a springtime pick-me-up, I reconnected with June's take on the traditional Easter bunny. Nicknamed "Marvy" lest he be confused with the movie star Harvey, five-foot-tall Marvy sat propped in the antique highchair used by Patrick and me and our four cousins. A light, flexible cotton rabbit, Marvy came upstairs from the basement and roved from room to room at Easter—a happy presence with his painted whiskered face and dressy vest. I reimagined my old Easter basket. Bunny-shaped chocolates, hopefully with nuts, nestled in colorful straw among dyed hardboiled eggs that June would soon devil. I sticky-fingered through jelly beans, securing every single purple bean just for me, setting aside red and black rejects for bartering with the inexperienced. One of my straw Easter hats, a black ribbon flowing from its crown and its brim stiff and wide, still hung from pegboard on a basement wall. Far from a proper Easter bonnet donned by some of my miserable friends, my homemade headdress was a winner.

Halloween wasn't entirely without merit—the merciful day after marked the start of November. Thanksgiving remained our all-round best one-day holiday—a day specifically set aside for gratitude and a celebratory feast savored with regular and first-time guests. June zoned the kitchen off limits as Thanksgiving prep commenced. The dining room table was set the day before, additional chairs angled in at corners and squeezed between table legs, its elegant appearance an open invitation. The rarely used Wedgewood place setting, complete with salad and bread plates, plus a careful lineup of sterling silver utensils lay on a pressed linen tablecloth with thick, fluffy linen napkins. Waterford goblets sparkled in sunlight. A ceramic turkey-emblazoned platter, empty for now, rested in the table's center between candles, along with a small Thanksgiving bell and delicate turkey-shaped salt and pepper shakers. The tinkling bell pronounced the feast ready, pots simmering on the stove and platters crowding the counters. Plum carved the turkey, chewing as she sliced, doling out samples. You could count on it. Turkey, stuffing with oysters and without, gravy in its special "boat" with its fancy curved ladle, fresh cranberries plus cranberry relish with walnuts, citrus, and cloves. Bibb lettuce with vinaigrette, green beans, Plum's biscuits, and her pumpkin and apple pies. June explained to any newbies that sauerkraut "cleanses the palate" while Mac kindly warned that turnips "taste like dirt." Big Daddy ate and listened, a silent chuckler. You could rest, assured.

Ah, but Christmas. More than a holiday, Christmas was the fifth season. Her joy contagious, my mother loved this time of year enough for everybody. Our first Christmas shortly after we moved into 1203 seemed a miracle. I posted lookout for the mailman at the front window in the living room, his truck delivering cards twice a day—people knew we lived here! Our first puppy crawled from a cardboard box on Christmas morning, an apartment promise kept. A black and white spaniel mix, Patches would spend a long life with us, always true to his nature—grouchy, stubborn, independent. What fun we enjoyed for weeks. Even the words for Christmas foods tickled me. Cheese straws and eggnog. Cheese balls, date balls, and bourbon balls. Wedding cookies (yum) and fruitcake (alas). I had yet to acquire a taste for my two favorite names—mincemeat pie and "Plum" pudding.

Wanting more Christmas, I headed to the basement. From his high chair, Marvy presided over the most higgledy-piggledy section of the basement where holiday trappings landed at the occasion's end. I crossed his lanky legs and surveyed his surroundings, then carried bin after Christmas bin into an open area near Mac's desk. Behind the just-emptied shelves hid a barely discernible Christmas tree stand. Having slipped out of sight, it was completely covered in cobwebs. I settled in my dad's swivel chair, poking inside random containers for mementos long unseen.

Looking through a box of ornaments, each one protected in a wad of newspaper, I came upon at least five copies of the *Richmond Times-Dispatch,* December 18, 1983. During home emptying I often stopped to read scraps of old newspapers, intrigued by these crumpling history leaflets, but I'd not come upon an entire paper intact. What happened on this date? I mimicked my dad at his desk, flipping through that Sunday's paper. National and local news, entertainment and sports, comics and a magazine. And the last segment—humdinger! A photograph of our kitchen dressed up for Christmas accompanied the featured article in the "Living Today" section. I encountered Mrs. Edward J. McCarty, an "area interior designer who has a portable pine mantel that she uses wherever," interviewed for her last-minute decorating tips—the mantel shown propped against the wall opposite the kitchen sink. Another photo showcased the ficus fig tree in the living room, adorned with miniature white lights and ornaments, wrapped presents scattered underneath. I saw anew my mother's touch at Christmas:

"Another quick trick on the living room mantel is a narrow, 2-foot-long fish platter piled high with pear, golden delicious and green apples, cedar and little votive candles. She also likes over-size crocks and baskets filled with magnolia, gingerbread men (you can buy them), and other greens, a big container of lemons and limes interspersed with green sprigs, a big bowl or basket filled with bell-shaped bite-size chocolates wrapped in red, green and silver foil. Mrs. McCarty also works with a friend turning the Little Sisters of the Poor lobby into an 18th century holiday room. Her friend lives in the country—a good thing if you're into greens."

A timeout taken for lunch, Billy and I relaxed in the living room. I paused at the sight of the ficus tree that I'd watered earlier. Its top branches now bent at the ceiling—could it be the one in the photograph? Sometimes I thought that 1203's personal "interior designer" was a titch over-the-top in her Christmas zeal. Rhythmically sidestepping as she carried her mantel around the house, experimenting with its placement—detailing the exact tree for Mac to fetch, checking his list twice. But she wasn't fickle in her love for the season, including the one that she knew would be her last. How bittersweet, that Christmas. While I decorated two tabletop trees for the front windows, the greens gatherer of yore napped in the den. Passing her a week later with boxes going to their post-Christmas basement storage area, I heard her knowing voice as she repeated her mantra, "yes, for next year." Lunch stuck in my throat. I needed a little Christmas past. Let's sit a spell longer, Billy, and deck some old halls.

For our early years at 1203, June positioned the tree in the living room by the banister, assuring that it would be the focal point—a Scotch pine visible halfway down the stairs, coming up the driveway, entering through the front door, opening the back gate. That-a-girl, I admired her knowhow now. Small white lights, never flickering, wound around branches. Keepsake yellowing cards snuggled into hollows. Strands of paper stars circled the tree, the oldest ornaments secured from hooks on out of the way branches. A pooch discovered water in the tree stand, this opportunity soon blocked by presents and Patrick's trainset. An angel perched at the pointy top. Over the years, the tree moved wherever June's whimsy directed. All comers for over a half century admired her tree, still aglow for New Year's Day, gifts of new ornaments welcomed.

My friend Jan in New Hampshire visited June for their annual taking-down-the-tree party, June explaining to me that they were "Christmas people." Like clockwork, Jan's wreath of Vermont greenery arrived every Christmas to brighten the back gate.

Mistletoe beckoned above doorways. Four slim, brass angels spun round and round, jingling on energy supplied by candles burning underneath. A soft white glow from one electric candle warmed each window. Reliving those days, I appreciated that, far from gaudy or commercial, Christmas décor at 1203 centered on nature's offerings and thrived on unchecked joy. I cued remembered Christmas music loud enough for Billy to hear. Andy Williams singing versions of "The Christmas Song" and "Most Wonderful Time of the Year," his scratchy album spinning on the pantry turntable. Mahalia Jackson intoning "Go Tell It on the Mountain" and "Hark! The Herald Angels Sing." Darlene Love belting the best "Winter Wonderland" and a horse whinny signaling a bouncy "Sleigh Ride" with the Ronettes. Judy Garland and Frank Sinatra trading versions of my favorite, "Have Yourself a Merry Little Christmas." Even as a kid, though, hearing the first note of this song could induce a quick lump in my throat. "Through the years we all will be together / If the fates allow." Not wanting to know, I knew for sure that in time the fates wouldn't allow—my youthful, carefree joy was imperiled. That truth hit home today.

The smells of Christmas overpowered July humidity, and I inhaled a unique combo of the fresh outdoors and seasonal good food. Bright green running cedar laps around the house—along the banister and living room and portable mantels, window sills and picture frames, shaping into garlands tied with red bows, draping over anything stationary from the antique clock to garden statues. Cloves prick oranges, peppermint sticks mix with pomegranates, pineapples ripen above the fireplace. The delicate look of paper whites belies their pungent odor. Wreaths fashioned from boxwood clippings, swags of fragrant pine branches full of cones, and red-berried holly hang from the front and back doors. And then the smell that summed up Christmas wafted over me—Mac McCarty's cranberry punch.

Mac periodically stirred and test-tasted his seasonal potion that brewed for hours in a humongous stockpot. Cranberries, oranges, and their fresh juices, plus cloves and nutmeg and cinnamon and who knows what else—he made several batches of his secret recipe over a weekend, pouring it through a sieve into bottles that he'd saved all year. We drank it piping hot in Christmas mugs painted with old carols and wintry scenes, blowing to cool and watching steam rise. Some evenings, Mac served kids and grownups from different bottles—the adult punch renamed a hot toddy. But the biggest fun lay in making home deliveries.

The satisfied brewer filled and corked glass bottles, tying ribbon around their necks. Mac labeled each one for a specific house call, sandwiching punch bottles between newspapers in cardboard boxes with cutout handles for easy carrying. Ready for takeoff, my dad tucked under his arm an empty Tole-painted tin box. Mac diligently plotted our route—we started at the house farthest away and worked our way back home. He calculated the time we could spend at each stop, immediately abandoning the schedule as soon as we arrived at the Miller residence on Ralston Road.

Three girls-a-waiting sat in the bay window—girls we first met during apartment days—the Millers' ground level pad my second home as I scurried down from the third floor. What a timeline of ongoing affection over sixty-five years, fortified by punch and brownies, refreshed in each season of our lives. Using the holidays as opportunities, we celebrated every occasion together in younger days—and later mourned together whenever the fates demanded. Today I yearned for that special stopover at their home, the one where the tin box would fill with brownies cut into squares, topped by confectioner's sugar. Old acquaintance, never forgot.

Done in, I dusted off the newly-recovered Christmas tree stand and set it among smaller ones "for next year." Billy and I, two old pals, sat on the front stoop and watched the sunset—a new adventure for us. I couldn't conceive of this home-emptying job without his trusty and trusting presence. On our daily walks during this summer of 2013, we met neighbors who befriended us. New acquaintance, now remembered. While I pined for the old days, I also felt reinvigorated by memories, high on life, pumped for days to come.

I focused on my favorite 1203 Christmas tree. Octogenarian June discovered it in an unattended lot—she had to have this very one and couldn't part with it. With the tree and without a second thought, she left a signed note stating that she'd be back. Her description of the attendant's incredulous, beaming face when she reappeared with cash in hand sums up the spirit of every holiday: "You came back!" he declared twice. "Good heavens, of course, I came back. Good heavens."

Despite the holiday emphasis on tradition, there's nothing outdated about coming back. It's the height of fashion, this perennial coming back, sustaining friendship and investing in relationships old and new. Here's to celebrating good will at every chance. Carry on and on.

Happy Fifth of July. Good heavens.

The Messenger Bag

Like playing nonstop hopscotch, my feet had moved un-characteristically fast in the days leading up to my mother's early May garden party. Searching the basement for flower vases to center each table, I noticed a brown leather satchel propped against the back of my dad's desk.

Etched on a brass plate, "E McCarty/USNR" identified the owner of the well-preserved messenger bag. I sat in his swivel chair, cradling his carrying case. Did he look through it often? I unhooked buckles and straps and peered inside. Whoa. This treasure trove deserved my undivided attention. I latched it securely for now. Clutching its sturdy single handle, I carried it upstairs to my bedroom, my discovery safe and only temporarily set aside.

At last, during my last week residing at almost empty 1203, I retrieved the messenger bag. At once, I gained entry into an old world brand new to me.

Far from alone in my old home, I was alive in a tumultuous decade shaped by war. Peeking randomly into each section, I caught glimpses of Mac's happy college days followed by draft orders to report for flight training. Several sections of the bag celebrated his courtship of my mother that began during lifeguarding summers at Virginia Beach and continued the rest of his life. Maps, telegrams, photos and more photos, letters, old newspapers—everything precisely arranged and separated by built-in dividers. I wanted to absorb it all immediately. I chose, however, to let his intimate story unfold my father's way—from the beginning.

Billy and I settled on the patio an hour before sunset, and I took flight on my trip back in time. The first dividers spotlighted Scholar McCarty's love for Washington and Lee University in Lexington, Virginia. Photographs, friends' names and campus locations noted on the back, introduced me to my father the college boy, a charmer decked out in bow tie and sport coat. His jolly-looking friends, also dressed to a tee, enchanted me. I wanted to read the titles of the books toted under their arms and finagle an introduction to the gent with thumbs hooked under his suspenders. How dashing, these lads in their two-toned shoes and flying scarves. I flipped through pages of detailed entries in a small spiral notebook—a ledger of Mac's careful budget as he worked full-time to pay for tuition and housing. I came upon a striking pencil drawing of my collegiate father tucked neatly into a notebook—a perfect profile likeness signed by "Hoffman."

Commencement mementos testified to his success as a cum laude graduate, a feat he accomplished in three years. Professors' praise lined the margins of his blue book exams, each page filled with Mac's neat penmanship in black ink. I chuckled at the wordiness of a suggestion written on an A paper on Chaucer: "It occurs to me that this might have undergone condensation in places with little damage to its overall quality." His Shakespeare mentor disclosed at the end of Mac's final exam dated May 31, 1941, that teaching him was the "supreme pleasure of this teacher's life." I reread every precious word. My dad's snappy writing reeled me in. He discerned similarities between Hamlet and Brutus, dissected Othello's character, probed Cleopatra's wily persona. At times, the willful Queen of the Nile interrupted Mac's learned prose. "There was always something doing when she was around...you might liken her to a good-time Charley!" A week later I retrieved my college blue books, and, as I expected, my Shakespeare exams read much like Mac's—rooting for Hamlet, fearing Lady Macbeth, and playing along with Puck—further evidence of our timeless father-daughter bond.

Daylight faded at a good stopping point. Puttering about the kitchen, I reflected on the guy I'd met tonight. What a jovial, handsome fellow stood at a diner's entrance, a flashing Schlitz beer sign overhead. My private investigation revealed a hardworking student devoted to his studies and his friends and duly rewarded with occasional socializing. My dad ever-inspired me with his love of learning. As soon as I was introduced to Shakespeare in ninth grade, Mac and I fell naturally into what became a lifelong hobby—we quoted the Bard, traded memorized passages, substituted different endings for his plays. I thought tonight of these verses from Sonnet 116, the one we loved best: "Love's not Time's fool, though rosy lips and cheeks / Within his bending sickle's compass come." Yes indeed, love defeated time's passage this evening. I strolled with my young father on the hilly grounds of W&L in 1942, recalling some years later our cherished trips to my prospective colleges. As we drove along, our conversations roamed freely from literature, dorm life, boys, sports, to the privilege of higher education. We both loved at first sight Hollins College, which lies not far from Washington and Lee and nestles in the same mountain range. Tonight, I read the printed program from his May 1942 baccalaureate service—he sang the hymn "O, God Our Help in Ages Past," just as I did, with him, at mine.

The messenger bag proved irresistible, sleuthing through its folders my nighttime indulgence. On consecutive rainy evenings, Billy and I swung on the sunporch glider while I relived summer days lifeguarding, sunbathing, and merrymaking at Virginia Beach. My parents' courtship began there and endured wartime separation. Piecing together the contents of several crammed sections of the messenger bag, I entered a world pulsing with vigor.

What fun I missed. Popping with humor, mischief, and promise, photographs crackle with a bold zest for life. Count me in! A tan lifeguard funding his college education, Mac laughs and chats from his stand, on the boardwalk, and at the shed where he rents floats and beach chairs. The grinning man—a whistle dangling from his neck and a foot resting against a rung of the lifeguard stand— would soon meet three beachcombers chatting in umbrella-shaded, blue canvas chairs. Look at those bathing beauties. Plum sometimes treated her two girls to brief getaways from Richmond to Virginia Beach. Snapshots shift quickly from Mac as popular lifeguard to Mac as permanent addition to the female trio.

How happy they were without me! I savored the smallest details of each photo, sure not to leave fingerprints, and relished spending these ocean days with them. Though money was tight and war breaking out, their intense pleasure in the here and now captivated me. I rode the waves, shared a sandwich, blew a kiss. Abundant photos record the courtship of my not-quite-yet father with his arm glued around a beaming gal named June. I stretched out with the foursome on beach towels, smelled the same salty air, and invented their conversations. Among his summer souvenirs, I uncovered a packet of telegrams and letters from author-philosopher Edgar Cayce's son Hugh that celebrate the friendships both Cayces formed at the beach with my father. Shortly before he died, Edgar foretold a fine life for the lifeguard whom he frequently observed carrying a man with polio into splashing ocean freedom. Now I grasped the significance, late in his life, of my dad's gift to me of Cayce's books.

I also had proof positive that I inherited my love for the sound and sight of crashing waves. Inhaling ocean air leaves me tipsy. Photos galore show my life-to-be rooted in the sand—salt water ran through my veins from the start. How beautiful, with the rain falling at 1203, that I could spend beach days with the people who loved me first—so alive, joyous, future-bound.

The mood of the messenger bag changed abruptly. Departing for military duty only days after his graduation, serviceman Mac and his girlfriend June now communicated long-distance. Wow, check out these boldly flirtatious letters, suggestive postcards, and slightly naughty inscriptions scribbled on the backs of photographs. I laughed aloud at the teasing phrases penned at the bottom of posed snapshots, reprints framed on his desk in Pensacola or her bureau in Richmond. Their frequent telegram exchanges demonstrated an uncommon ability to say a lot in a few expensive words. Two folded telegrams concealed a receipt inside. First telegram, June to Mac: "No mail. Worried about you. What is wrong." Next, to Mac's unknown response, June replied: "Impossible to marry that early but please come anyway." Hah! Perhaps Mac gave up on telegrams—on January 18, 1944, E. McCarty paid $8.10 to wire a dozen red roses "to the one I love," the same girl he married on February 7.

The receipt for the roses, folded inside the telegrams, confirmed delivery by Richmond's Fuqua and Sheffield florist. What a coincidence. A generation later my high school pals and I hoped for prom corsages from this florist and pleaded with our parents to fetch our dates' boutonnieres there. Surely one of this throwback shop's most gorgeous ever arrangements appeared in 1991 on the front stoop, delivered to 1203 when Mac died—flowers chosen just for him by my kindergarten through high school friend Betsy.

With only the satchel's last few dividers left to explore, I sought the comfort of Mac's favored chair in the living room. I rested my head on the tall back. In a stiff brown envelope addressed to Edward James McCarty, stark draft orders command this light-hearted fellow report for military duty on June 6, 1942. I pictured his hands holding these papers. I ran my fingers around the edges, getting as close to him as possible. The shocking about-face from the bag's college and beach day memorabilia to its messages of war overpowered me. My heart sank with my father's heart, with the heart of everyone touched by this nightmare.

Until I discovered the messenger bag, the wartime photos that I'd seen captured Mac and his mates in their flight school barracks or socializing in Pensacola. Quite a few show the new lieutenant in his dress white uniform visiting his crew of Richmond girls. He wore formal dress blues on his wedding day. Today I experienced firsthand why Mac didn't talk with me about the War. He saw no need. And I never asked—I saw no need. But he spoke now, crystal clear, through his keepsakes.

Newspaper headlines frightened me still, enormous blackened letters conveying the horror of the December 7, 1941 attack on Pearl Harbor. Photos showed the recent liberal arts student in pursuit of another kind of education at flight school in Pensacola. Coat and tie traded in for flight jacket and goggles, Mac and friends I would never know stood tall in aviator gear outside barracks and in the breathtakingly small landing zone on an aircraft carrier. I marveled at their smiles for the camera. Soon enough, still smiling Lieutenant McCarty and his proud crew posed for a more formal photograph, the tail of their plane in the background—my father's handwriting listing names and hometowns of enlisted personnel on the back. Anxious and fearful all these years later, I touched a heavy object lying by itself at the bottom of one section. Ah, now I would understand the surprising weight of the messenger bag.

I rubbed the texture and contours of a brown suede pouch approximately nine inches tall and four and a half inches wide. Another, darker suede pocket within protected an "Aerial Dead Reckoning Computer" and a protractor for taking measurements on the handheld "computer." Using only this basic equipment—a metal dial, covered in measurements, twisted left or right over a graph behind it which was filled with even more lines and numbers—my pilot father and his co-pilot calculated coordinates via "Altitude and

Airspeed Computations." Mac's still legible pencil dots pinpoint the location of the target. Such an unfathomable, unavoidable responsibility. What was the crew's assignment? How did these young chaps summon the courage for these "operations?" Not only was the "reckoning computer" hard for me to trust, but the plane resembled an airborne jalopy—photos snapped from the rear of the cockpit showed dilapidated chairs and pedals, tiny windshield wipers, and two half-moon-shaped steering wheels.

Just as words failed my dad, my imagination failed me. I stopped reading and sat. Enough for one night, I thought, and too much for any lifetime. Mac's silence about wartime had taught me to be extra-sensitive to my college students returning from tours of combat duty. I recalled his wordless anxiety when his nephew Daniel, a Marine Lieutenant, departed for Beirut immediately after the 1983 barracks bombing. My dad, way out of character, remained mostly grumpy and preoccupied until Daniel's safe return.

A generation later Thomas, Daniel's youngest child, developed keen interest in military history. From a photocopy of Mac and his crew, Thomas identified the plane, partially visible, in the background—a "Consolidated PB2Y Coronado." From that tidbit, the promising researcher outlined possible scenarios of Mac's tour of duty in the Pacific. "I'm absolutely sure that in October 1944 he was transferred to VH-1, a maritime rescue squadron. Those seaplanes rescued a lot of aircrew. I bet that gave your dad some peace. I hear he was really nice." And I'm certain that Mac would have preferred conversing with Thomas about their mutual passion for Greek and Roman philosophy.

Only two sections left, I returned to the armchair, longing for evidence of better days. A rubber band bound the Lieutenant's release papers. Whew. I recognized the man who responded to a December 31, 1946 letter informing him that he owed the US Treasury $28.00—the Navy overpaid his per diem from November 7-13, 1945, granting him $7.00 rather than the allotted $3.00. My father's detailed mathematical reply tickled me with its explanation of the amount that the Navy owed him. I didn't find the resolution but bet on Mac the future banker.

As I imagined the relief and joy surrounding his homecoming, suddenly I heard my mother's voice. I set aside the last papers for the moment, picturing her face as she confided in me years after my father died. Wartime didn't end for him until he fulfilled a self-imposed final duty. Mac and June embarked on a road trip to meet with families of crew members who died under his command. June waited in the car while Mac shook hands with those waiting for him at the door, and she joined him when he accepted an invitation for coffee or lunch. Returning to the car, a map on the dashboard tracing the route to their next destination, they drove on without comment. Only after completing this trip could he set out on his career, June tenderly concluded. Searching now for that photograph of the crew before flight, I studied with new eyes the names and hometowns on the back.

Oh, how great the burdens placed on a recent college boy separated from the girl he loved, an only child also responsible for his mother. What resilience shown by Mac, his crew, and the Richmond women devoted to him. They offer a comforting reminder that I, too, if strong-willed, can rise to any occasion. And I'll choose happiness, no matter what, just like my beach-loving role models.

Mac's inner serenity—ocean-given wisdom likely garnered while gazing at the horizon from his lifeguard stand—held fast, stronger than his unspoken grief. How right that he's remembered for his instinctive empathy. He always gave everyone the benefit of the doubt—no one knows what sorrow burrows in another heart. I pick up the tenor of his voice, greeting me hello or bidding me farewell with a shout of "Peace, Baby."

I opened the messenger bag's last manila folder and stared long and hard at unbelievable paperwork. Impossible! Holy Moly

Billy Willy. The icing on my home-emptying summer's cake.

At the exact time that "E. McCarty/USNR" reported for duty in the summer of '42, construction workers hammered away at the fourth residence on a secluded, tree-enveloped, dead-end street in the then far West End of Richmond, Virginia. Events conspired to bring us all home to this house on a hill in the winter of 1957.

Peace, Dad.

1203 Now

August 8, 2013. Billy and I would bid 1203 farewell this afternoon.

Yesterday, Billy's heart broke. The steadiest pup all summer, he'd nipped frantically at movers' heels as they carried my mother's chair out the front door. Notoriously strong-jawed, he clenched the chair's skirt between his teeth, his white body dragging along the pine floor like a fifth leg. I picked up the saddest dog in 1203 history. He barked in vain until the chair disappeared. Billy gave up and collapsed his head on my shoulder, his furry noggin snuggled between my neck and chin. Two broken hearts.

I checked each empty room with a baseball-sized lump in my throat, examining every deep closet and hidden nook. Billy's nails clicked on bare pine floors. My flipflops shuffled to repeated standstills. Funny how the emptied house felt just like home. I sensed the vacant rooms filling. Family and friends walked with me in spirit.

All clear inside. Billy stretched out on the cool back stoop, head on his front paws and big brown eyes taking in every last detail of his world. I returned to the exact spot where I'd rested on May 5, the day after June's garden sendoff. Holiest smoke and major boo-yah. How did I get *here* from *there?* I retraced the summer of my life.

Three months younger but not wiser, I had sat on this same white bench on the patio still shaded by the elegant party tent. I faced my home-emptying job, straight-up honest and downright overwhelmed. Sitting and relaxing smacked of 1203 comfort food as I contemplated the physical and emotional road ahead. I hung out, unworried but not carefree. Admiring the flower box under the kitchen window, I replayed a favorite scene from college years. "You have no idea how much this eggbeater is worth," my mother stated correctly, shaking her head and the beater my way. Red and white paint chipped off its handle and crank, blades dull with traces of rust, I smiled as its whirring sound gained speed in her hand. Decades later, in 2013, I learned that eggbeater's value.

Our one-way eggbeater exchange symbolized my mother's suspicion that physical objects didn't mean much to her daughter, unless sentiment bound me forever to Raggedy Ann, Converse tennis shoes, or a patchwork quilt. My childhood dislike of downtown shopping trips never dimmed, a pigtailed girl begrudgingly exchanging shorts and tee shirt for frilly dress and patent leather Mary Janes (with ankle socks!). Lucky that my all-afternoon frown didn't leave permanent creases, I scuffed those shiny black shoes up and down escalators at Thalhimers and Miller & Rhoads department stores, glared into window displays at Montaldo's and Schwarzchild's, and pointed out every big clock whose hands surely signaled time to go. I couldn't have known what a treat such excursions were for Plum and her daughters, an always frugal trio with eyes trained to spot a bargain. I did not care, not one iota.

When my mother entrusted me with responsibility for 1203's emptying, one that I know she imagined, what did she foresee? Yes, she had designated a few dear items here and there. Since college graduation, furnishings from 1203 had transformed all my dwellings into homes—cobbler's benches and rocking chairs, end tables and braided rugs, all simple things creating a sense of place. But this was different. Every decision was now mine.

Not long before she died, my mom and I walked arm-in-arm around our old home as she inquired what I'd like for mine. She so enjoyed the image of certain things, cherished and chosen by us together, leaving 1203 for good with me when that day came—the brass candlesticks from Rome, a tavern table with saw-buck base for my kitchen, and the flat back cupboard and dry sink that have been my lifelong companions. She envisioned two paintings, one hanging in each bedroom, and suggested their right-as-always placement.

But what should, what would I do with everything else? What could satisfy my mother like picturing the candlesticks on my mantel? And not only all the things, but what to do with my heart?

How I remember that May afternoon when I left 1203 empty of its people for the first time, heading down the driveway with chipper Billy bound for his Charlottesville home. I returned as the official and clueless home emptier a week later, without a plan but with resolve and my canine assistant. These hour-long commutes between Charlottesville and Richmond, interspersed with overnights and weekend stays, would end in August.

Who could have predicted that beauty and joy would triumph over hard labor and unmatched sadness—that June's request would turn into my privilege? I was in uncharted waters with no expectations. Yet even at the outset, I never questioned my somewhat mysterious but surefire trust in the outcome.

Weeks passed. I stood in the kitchen on the first workday since all my family members had taken their chosen objects from

1203. Despite all the takeaways from each room, the house remained full. Now what? As I gazed around the kitchen I knew by heart, I glanced at one of June's friends gently running her fingers over a platter's scalloped edges. "Would you like it?" I asked without thinking. Her pure pleasure touched me and I heard myself offer "Would you like it?" more frequently to enthusiastic responses. Yes, to the cut-glass celery dish. Of course, to the rolling pin. I've always coveted Southern ladies' tablecloths, may I?

I waded into this new phase of my task cautiously but confident that the way through was opening to its own beat. "Is there anything you'd like from 1203?" I proposed to all those pitching in to help, their friends and family members joining the effort, and neighbors and their pals popping in with food. Progress in fits and starts, a box packed and a bag filled, one foot in front of the other, still without a definitive plan, until in a flash, my epiphany.

There was only one right thing to do. Only one answer as to how to clear out the loved home suited the place. Only one way of emptying 1203 honored all who played their parts.

I gave it all away.

Hadn't everyone given it all away, all along—talent, commitment, sacrifice, kindness, love? Wasn't generosity of spirit what we shared with each other and the reason that guests soon felt at home, in their home, at 1203? Isn't that why I invited friends home for sleepovers, basement romps, a cookout, any holiday? Weren't the four of us the beneficiaries of so many unsought gifts and unasked help through the years, from azalea bushes to hand-me-down school uniforms to generator hookups when the power failed? How about the unlimited time freely donated by my home-emptying helpers, such big-hearted commitments the epitome of housewarming? Isn't giving the marrow of *home?*

What an abrupt about-face for me, the perpetually reluctant shopper. Each and every thing in the house now mattered—it had been part of the whole, a piece of the tapestry that took almost sixty years to weave. Little things at 1203 possessed immeasurable value—that (forlorn) sewing kit, misshapen thimble, lunchbox with thermos bracket inside, wooden spoon, night light. This mohair scarf, green "depression glass" vase, scarab bracelet, decanter, pewter pitcher. Those napkin rings, coasters, watering cans, decorations, salt and pepper grinders—their "prices" couldn't be named. Money was no good here—invaluable took on true meaning. Yes, things mattered, but only because they served as tokens for all the lives that rubbed up against each other over fifty-six years. You can't buy relationship. You don't pay for gifts.

Day in and day out, room by room, I touched or looked at every single thing, buoyed by volunteers showing up at just the right time. A daily rhythm bounced around the house and yard, laughs far outnumbered tears, an instant camaraderie shared by no longer strangers. It was just like old times, this last time.

For my farewell party at 1203—a long one over three months—the house bustled with life, plenty of play and goofiness, and at times that sweet old happiness. Stories of others' memories warmed me—a nostalgic explanation of what touched them about the teapot or timer on the stove—and newcomers to 1203 met my family as they wrapped up in Plum's shawl and buttoned June's trench coat. I floated on a dawning awareness of new relationships forming on top of the old ones—things finding homes where they would be part of fresh memories. Like the hands of teammates stacked first one, then another, on top of each other to rest on a basketball before tipoff, these new relationships piled on top of the old ones. I locked it all down, safe in memory's eye.

I unlocked it now.

A talkative duo strides up the basement stairs, Floyd's head thrown back in Mac's straw beach hat and his sidekick Chris in a fedora cocked at a rakish angle. Making many trips through the back door, an expert packer loads her car with a 1203 makeover kit for her hair salon—newly upholstered wingback chairs in her waiting area, a bench at a bay window, an orchid and magazines on a pie stand, and a mirror for a before and after look tops off Susan's renovation. Teenagers fill boxes to stock their grandma Janet's kitchen and pantry, "crazy-excited" about tonight's feast baked in the "gigantic" lasagna pan, Peewee and Diamond passing Billy from lap to lap as they work. What would I have done without these four nimble-legged kids trotting up and down steps, making everyone's work easier, storing their memories of this unusual summer camp? They opted to take away small, personal mementos—book, snow globe, framed photo of Billy. May thoughts of our good times linger. A neighbor's daughter and friend shriek while modeling glad rags, vintage clothes straight from June's closet, and debate where to show off their outfits. A first-time visitor spots a cake stand, proudly reporting that his daughter wins the baking award every year at the West Virginia State Fair. Hours later he heads home with teary thanks and her first "proper" cake stand.

The ceramic monkey above the kitchen sink rides shotgun in a pickup truck to his new perch overlooking the Piankatank River. Parents squeeze "new" beds and dressers into vehicles lined up in the driveway. Bartering handymen alternate picks of tools. Weighted-down passenger vans set out to deliver badly needed items wherever, anywhere. Miniature portraits of four Gibson girls depart for another bathroom wall. Martini glasses trade one handsome bartender's home for another. A talented massage therapist walks away with a framed photo for his studio, his predecessor Plum the masseuse bent over her table. "Now I know the meaning of priceless," he whispers. A French professor jollies up her office with a Parisian watercolor. Cheerful artwork lightens the burden for patients in the waiting room. A moving van transports surprises to Jan's New Hampshire home, one box packed with special care and labeled "do not open till Christmas" for June's partner in December fun. Watching the huge vehicle navigate its way down the hill, I picture the big Heflebower truck following us up the gravel drive in 1957.

Someone exclaimed at June's garden party, "1203 is everybody's home." Countless places already make me feel right at home again—this deep-down-delight an unanticipated bonus of giving it all away. The most homesick child in the world, from my first sleepover all the way through college and whenever I headed down the driveway toward my own "home," I can go home again and again, near and far, the stories picking up steam. And magically, 1203 spins beyond my reach or awareness in its effortless way. Isn't this "not knowing" who sits at my childhood desk also exhilarating? What birds flock to which feeders I know not where? Who looks back from bedroom mirrors now? 1203 ripples far.

"Home again, home again, jiggety-jig." A young bride wears her friend June's bracelet, its rubies glinting in the sun. 1203 mainstay Amy-Daniel decorates her first principal's office with a Japanese print, and her daughter puts away clothes in a dresser splashed with hand-painted strawberries. A tennis buff jogs through Richmond neighborhoods, decked out in June's hooded Rafael Nadal sweatshirt. College students knot Mac's ties on graduation day. Jonathan wears his uncle's cufflinks for luck. Matthew rolls around on the swivel chair from that huge desk in the basement. Maria sports June's beret and listens for the well-known clunk of three bells on her own garden gate. Plum's great-granddaughter Madeleine strums her ukulele as her son-in-law Roger receives physical therapy on her massage table. "Home again, home again, jiggety-jog."

And you bet I took that eggbeater—it hums "not for sale." Those pieces chosen by my mother and me center my home. The sleigh bells switched back doors, now announcing arrivals on my patio for Billy to greet. What else? Raggedy Ann and an old quilt, the magnifying glass I wrongly couldn't foresee using, board games with the Scrabble tiles in the tattered brown bag, garden gloves with holey fingers, ceramic planters, a picnic basket with ribbons streaming from the handles, legal pads from my dad's desk. I share heart-shaped rocks from June's collection while vigilant for ever more. The "kiss of the sun" plaque nestles among flowing grasses, rocks, and jonquils in my garden. Mac's US NAVY blanket heats the whole house. His messenger bag, softened by leather conditioner, remains organized as he left it, except for my framing of his likeness sketched by a college friend. June's songs and Plum's short stories lie in wait, ready for prime time. My three baseball bats lean against a wall. I pluck one to swing at the drop of a pen.

So that's how it happened—three months from there in May to here in August. I sat up perfectly straight, struck full-force by beauty.

While serving as emptier-in-residence, I pocketed the keys to good living. 1203 taught me true. I'm clinging for the rest of my life to these gems recovered this summer.

Sit and listen, serenity waits in silence. Foster hospitality and storytelling—gather round and break bread over good conversation. Stoke the fires of courage and resilience. Persist regardless. Lean in with sensitivity, no matter what. Grab a dab of gumption and get on with it. Say yes to adventure. Write a book. Make humor a best friend forever—it never fails—belly-laugh in the mirror. Humility points out the high road—take it every time. Relax in comfortable companionship. Give time. Take time. Savor a lazy day. Work hard but stay un-busy. Set out fearless and free. Gobble up simple pleasures. Pack picnics. Fire up the grill. Forget dollar signs—measure value with the heart. Let kindness and generosity win each day. Play. Plant deep roots in nature—hustle outside. Dig and swim. Care.

Choose happiness. Love life and live it full up.

Invest all the way. Relationships last long, longer than time's reach.

I should throw my arms skyward and touch the moon each night, steeped in gratitude for everyone who made my life possible.

That grateful heart will ensure empathy and joy.

Thank you, beloved brick teacher on a hill.

Oh, Billy. Time's up here. We're leaving 1203.

I deadheaded plants, filled birdfeeders and birdbaths, swept the patio, grabbed Billy's leash from the stoop railing, packed a few last things in the car. Recognizing the opening notes of a hymn ringing out from the nearby carillon, I snapped out of my dawdling ways. That one song, of all songs, soaring over 1203 at this moment and for the first time in my memory? "How sweet the sound."

Gumption time. I patted the kitchen counter, closed the door behind me, latched the back gate, and lifted Billy into the car. Strains of an old tune saluted our departure, those splendid church bells pealing "Amazing Grace."

On the drive back to Charlottesville I reached for the windshield wipers, laughing through my tears at the sunny day. These tears, triggered by beauty, dropped like beads from my eyes. I've caught a lot of breaks in my life, but none compares to this opportunity to stop, to turn, and to look back at all the lives entwined at 1203, to appreciate them, together and alone, in their fullness. Everyone did their best.

As the chronicler of this time, I conclude that all is well. Everyone is young and healthy. The world is as ever full of promise—our lives, wrapped up in so many other lives then and now, still rich in love. Good rises, stretches, expands.

"And grace will lead us home."

Postscript

Who lives at 1203 now?

Our next-door neighbor asked if she could bring a friend over to see the house, which she did on the day after June's May 4 garden party. Amy loved the yard, gardens, and every quirky thing about the simple, well-built home. No central air or dishwasher, no problem. Pine floors need refinishing, paint flaking here and there, okay. She submitted her bid and we buyer and seller rookies did our best, home inspectors coming and going as the home emptied. No lockbox, not here. Many crossed fingers unglued on July 31 as Amy signed her name on various documents while wearing one of June's bracelets. A video of this marquee event streamed my cheering, crying way. At last Amy had her dream house, the first for her and her two teenage boys. She helped all summer—bringing empty boxes and lifting heavy ones, providing lunch, displaying unfailing compassion and gratitude. Though they never met, she remembers passing June on the driveway.

At Amy's request, patio furniture remains much the same, as do some birdfeeders and garden statues, plus things intentionally left as surprises for her within drawers, on banisters, in basement and garage. The back stoop hosts the tin milkbox with a slightly newer broom, both still overseen by the painted heart. What a treat to receive current photographs of the yard, the azaleas wild with color, or the sun reflecting off the stained glass at the top of the stairs. Jan still sends the fragrant Vermont Christmas wreath each year, another new friendship resting comfortably atop the old. Amy and I visit often. I've waited until I finish writing this book to go back to 1203, until then securing my remembrance. She arrives at my Charlottesville door with flowers plucked from the yard I love.

Amy of 1203 makes a great friend, each of us competing for which one of us is luckier. (I am.) Though Amy has yet to hear the bells perform "Amazing Grace."

A Primer on Home Emptying
Prepping for the Big Job

Many circumstances may conspire to make your project especially difficult —time constraints, geographic distance, financial worries, family bickering or worse, physical ailments, conflicts with other commitments, a broken heart. Know that I dealt with obstacles from start to finish—some days, it seemed difficulty had my number on speed dial. Still, you can take ownership of this experience, hold fast to its positive aspects, and seize opportunities.

At first, I had no answer for the many people asking how I emptied 1203 relatively quickly, while also staying attentive to details and careening on an emotional rollercoaster. I learned on the fly, no prior experience or advice. Now I understand how it all went down. Here are hard-earned suggestions for anyone touched by home emptying.

While your situation may vary dramatically from mine, emptying any home requires grit, perseverance, mental clarity, imagination, and senses of humor and fair play. Kindness and maturity win the long days, but sprinkle each one with horseplay and relaxation. Flat-out accepting your job is a must—no matter what happens, simply rise to the occasion. If you embrace this responsibility as an opportunity, you'll find it easier, uniquely meaningful, and forever memorable. It's a chance to round out your life and to gain a full-bodied understanding of some of your closest connections.

If even remotely possible, give yourself time and space for rest before beginning this job. Big changes brought this unwelcome task your way. Whatever the reasons, it's painful to leave a loved home for the last time. Remember that people everywhere worried as you worry, felt devastated and immobilized, yet survived and returned whole to their familiar lives. Don't ignore how you feel. Fully experiencing your emotions allows you to move through them, slowly, toward eventual healing. Stay true. Breathe.

Allow yourself to be overwhelmed. It's overwhelming! You've added a big job to the customary rhythm of your life. Indulge in fleeting thoughts of running away. Picture the island or mountaintop. Don't dive in willy-nilly, doing something here, another there, forgetting this, ignoring that. Do nothing at first. If doing something would help your morale, collect boxes. Label and stack them. Collect more. Write names of family and friends on some boxes. Set aside sizes suitable for specific items already promised. Collect more boxes.

I set my sights on a hoped-for completion week—longstanding professional obligations awaited me at the end of August. All my helpers knew the target week, too, and I see in retrospect that a deadline subconsciously figured in some of my decisions and worked to our advantage. A goal, though not set in stone, lends structure and purpose. And even if you don't meet the subjective deadline, a timeframe gives an inkling of how long the project will take—you can look back at what's been accomplished and lean forward into what's left. When you're closing in on your goal, glimpses of the finish line motivate like nothing else. And yes, the boon of a closing date for sale of 1203 proved a whopping incentive. The best planning remains guesswork, of course, so don't let your goal loom too large—lo, my helpers and I finished two weeks ahead of our ambitious goal.

Figure out when you're ready—progress depends on your ability to focus. Though you labor hard, if not clear-sighted you'll see no tangible results and create even more work. This job drains mentally, emotionally, physically. Put a stop to any mounting frustration—steady as you go, prepare as if for the final exam, tiptoe into your new workplace.

Sharpen pencils. Make lists. On your mark, get set. Go out to dinner. Tomorrow the work days commence—shorter ones at first, longer days as the way through opens.

Most importantly, find a dog like Billy.

Getting 'Er Done

Commit to the concept and practice of "Singletasking." Lay out a modest plan for the day and stay with it best you can. One small thing at a time, done thoroughly and completed, then the next, unhurried and deliberately. Multitasking spells disaster—the flurry increases chaos without achieving much progress. The scattered "approach" makes the job more difficult than it is. Don't deviate from the singletasking way when someone asks for another job. Stay the course. Start small. Today, the pantry and only the pantry—today books and only books—today the bathrooms—today the first day for this section of this side of the basement, and likely the next few days as well—this week the garage. Be flexible, but even if you alter your plan, singletask. "All right but take everything down only from that one cupboard. Only. Promise."

Delegate wisely. Consider your helpers' interests and talents. Convert everyone to the singletasking philosophy. Ask for suggestions—listen to fresh ideas. Think throughout the process about including other people. You'll be surprised who might come to mind and how much they will appreciate your invitation. Who spent holidays in your home? Who sent your parents birthday cards without fail?

Set aside letters, photo albums, anything that deserves your undistracted, unlimited time. Store them until the moment is right. Give the postcard, clipping, or scrapbook its due.

At day's end, you'll sometimes feel discouraged by a house that shows few signs of emptying. Fatigue triumphs, temporarily. But you'll be pleasantly surprised the next day, invigorated by the sight of your overall progress. Keep good faith. As space appears, and it will, your path presents itself more easily—you can better map out a doable day's work with a given number of helpers. Continue to singletask. Don't panic. Recognize when to stop. Stop. Call it a day despite the half-done list. Eat. Drink. Easy does do it.

Don't overload a session. You want to pay attention, concentrate, so that you don't miss it: a photograph pressed between magazine pages, a note taped to the bottom of a pitcher, a belt fallen behind the radiator. You're only going to have this chance once, so give it your all. Clear your mind with a walk, a leisurely chat, and go out for lunch. Pause and refresh.

Always have food and drinks at-the-ready. Accept everything offered—someone will be hungry. At day's end, leftovers transform into carry-out orders for tired workers.

Stop and take a break whenever anyone wants to share their findings. Listen attentively. Everyone involved is likely remembering cherished moments and relationships as they help you on your own journey. Kids think about their futures. Sudden longing strikes grownups of all ages, missing their parents anew when spotting an old Valentine card, box kite, or fishing pole. Empathy lightens all loads. Hear the new stories evoked by the old coffee mug or Christmas ornament. Storytelling filled my emptying days with joy.

Encourage everyone to look around. Ask and ask. What would you like? Would your grandchild enjoy the little rocker? Need pliers? Like that lamp? Encourage everyone to say repeatedly, "I'd love to have it."

Now. Ask again and again—do you have a friend who'd like this or that? Happiness spreads and the house empties as your helpers carry "gifts" to their cars and trucks. New homes for old things—suggest today's workers bring a friend tomorrow, to lend a hand and take away vintage shoes, snow shovels, scissors. Be bold.

Talk about it as you work or share lunch—friends with newborns, adult kids putting down a deposit on first apartments, family members and colleagues who likely know someone with immediate needs—it's amazing the good uses you'll find for so many things. Check with an organization such as United Way or Habitat for Humanity, contact a church or mosque or synagogue sponsoring outreach programs, and be sensitive to specific areas struck by recent catastrophe where residents wait for help. Investigate local charities. A teacher will probably know a family desperate for boxes of clothes and an after-school program itching for sports equipment and chess sets. Unfortunately, everyone knows someone in need. Rooms in a trailer cooled for the first time with a window unit from 1203. Other treasure fulfilled the entire wish list on several wedding registries. Actors at the neighborhood high school now strut about in hoop skirts, feathered hats, and tattersall vests. Ask around—and around it goes.

Let emotions come, come what may, as the end approaches.

The Afterglow

Oooooweeeeeee—the depth and breadth of home emptying emotions surface, ebb and flow, and linger—I continue to remember and learn. The lessons of those days—swinging back and forth between breath taking and thanks giving, tears and laughter, loss and gain—gradually return in clear-eyed memory. Tune into the show, absorb it all, from first day mayhem to last day leave taking.

Reflect at your leisure—when traveling, walking, gardening, listening to birds. Move forward into a lighter future, leaving behind old regrets or grievances, sustained by the relationships forged under that one roof. Hold tight, with a relaxed grip, to everything that propels you forward. Appreciate your enhanced understanding of people and events. Develop your newfound inner strengths—how about your capacity for endurance, ability to think on tired feet, and willingness to ask for help? You completed your job.

How life-affirming and changing this last trip home again. How invaluable, this instructive, bittersweet, beautiful farewell.

Thanksgiving

Full of 1203 spirit, the good times continued during the process of the home on a hill becoming a book. My dedicated collaborators worked and played in communal joy. As host of this making-of-a-book party, I celebrate another festive 1203 Thanksgiving, my cronies and I crowded around the dining room table. Candles lit. Billie Holiday sings "I Get a Kick Out of You." Frosty champagne glasses up. Clink!

Guests of Honor

Cameron Krest, agent and engineer, my ally and teacher, honest and kind, smart and humble, tried and true.

Kay Bethea, my one-of-a-kind editor, an imaginative dramatist and grammatical taskmaster, the theater-goer who assured that every reader could play a part in 1203's story.

Dan Meador, sensitive reader and my finetuning advisor, keen listener and the marathoner who ran with me all the way home.

Eleanor Garges Maxwell, my college roommate and deluxe statistician who still dances in the kitchen, a girl so at home at 1203 that she married the boy at 1210.

Andrew Kaufman, the sole member of my writing group and monthly breaker of bread over free-flowing conversations.

Roger Cunningham, my "no worries" graphic designer, creative and full-of-heart, who made this book a sparkling reality. And museum curator **Dan Mason** who offered his artistic vision, along with cover photographer **David Heald** who captured the moment.

Chefs
Jan Kilfeather-Mackey, Jeannette Purrington Twomey, Mary Katharine Froehlich, Meredith Cole, Christopher Gleason, Susan Mortell, Madeleine McCarty Mudd, and Tess Keena.

Caterers
Marguerite Steiber, Kristen Brooking Knies, Carol Dawson Fassio, Susan Johnson, Julie Gronlund, Cathy Strause Plotkin, and Lanetta Ware.

Clean-Up Crew
Brett Streiter, Kim Jenkins, Peter Bower, Martha Lankford, and Feline Floyd who came into the warmth.

1203 Movers and Shakers, Summer 2013
Thank you to all my helpers in lovingly emptying 1203 and filling my heart every day. A special sweaty salute to faithful friends Amy Gillespie and Susan Johns, traveling with me to and from Charlottesville, heavy lifting and light laughing all the way. And to Floyd Miller and Becca Beazley, waiting for me in Richmond and already on the job, along with Janet Johnson and her four fleet-footed grandchildren.

Past and Future Soulmates
Carolyn Jones (of 1205), Nancy Miller, and Barbara McCreary, who reminisced with me.

Amy Campbell, living at 1203 now and loving it like an old-timer, a compassionate woman who gave me a seamless and satisfying leave-taking as she joined the team like a basketball-playing sister.

Billy G. McCarty, my canine partner for eighteen years, three months, and six days. You took care of two McCarty women, June for thirteen years and me for five—a big job completed paw-perfectly. Your body stretches out full length in my heart and your spirit keeps me spry.

Next time we meet, I'll toss you the moon to fetch.
We'll sit on your old back stoop and munch stardust treats.

About the Author

Marietta McCarty is the author of New York Times Extended List Bestseller *Little Big Minds: Sharing Philosophy with Kids,* Nautilus Book Gold Award winner *How Philosophy Can Save Your Life: 10 Ideas That Matter Most,* and *The Philosopher's Table: How to Start Your Philosophy Dinner Club—Monthly Conversation, Music, Recipes.*

After spending a happy, studious, tennis-playing childhood in Richmond, Virginia, Marietta graduated from Hollins University and earned her Master's in philosophy from the University of Virginia. She taught the arts of clear thinking and good conversation for over two decades at Piedmont Virginia Community College in Charlottesville, Virginia. Now a writer by trade, she keeps her eye on the prize of good living through teaching and learning, speaking and listening, paying attention and loving the world. Pieces of 1203 reside with her at her home in Charlottesville.

For more from Marietta, visit her online at
www.mariettamccarty.com